JACK and NORMAN

ALSO BY JEROME LOVING

Confederate Bushwhacker

Mark Twain

The Last Titan

Walt Whitman

JACK and NORMAN

A State-Raised Convict and the Legacy of Norman Mailer's *The Executioner's Song*

Jerome Loving

Thomas Dunne Books
St. Martin's Press
New York

THOMAS DUNNE BOOKS.
An imprint of St. Martin's Press.

For information, address St. Martin's Press, 175 Fifth Avenue,
New York, N.Y. 10010.

www.thomasdunnebooks.com
www.stmartins.com

The Library of Congress Cataloging-in-Publication Data is
available upon request

ISBN 978-1-250-10699-5 (hardcover)
ISBN 978-1-250-10700-8 (e-book)

Our books may be purchased in bulk for promotional,
educational, or business use. Please contact your local
bookseller or the Macmillan Corporate and Premium Sales
Department at 1-800-221-7945, extension 5442, or by e-mail
at MacmillanSpecialMarkets@macmillan.com.

First Edition: February 2017

10 9 8 7 6 5 4 3 2 1

To the memory of

David C. MacNeill (1882–1980)

and

James J. Loving, Jr. (1908–80)

Contents

An awful lot of people are going to resent this book and they're going to say there's something just swinish about glorifying a two-time killer and a bad man, and I'm not certain that you can defend yourself against that absolutely.[1]

—NORMAN MAILER

Introduction

Early on the morning of Saturday, July 18, 1981, some-time between 5:00 and 6:00 A.M., two men would quarrel in a restaurant. Apparently, the dispute was over the use of the bathroom at the former Binibon Café, an all-night joint on the corner of East Fifth Street and Second Avenue in the then seedy East Village of Manhattan. Both individuals were artists. Richard Adan, managing his father-in-law's restaurant, was an émigré of Cuba and an aspiring playwright. Jack Henry Abbott, who had been recently released from prison after twenty years, hoped to immigrate to Cuba and was the author of the newly published *In the Belly of the Beast: Letters from Prison*. Adan had yet to make his mark as an artist but was on his way. Abbott, who had taught himself to write in prison, had just produced a bestseller. *The New York Times Book Review* for the next day printed an ecstatic appraisal, which New Yorkers would wake up to read before they heard the very latest news about the author.

The men quickly moved their argument outside, where Adan tried to calm the waters by showing Abbott a place behind a Dumpster where he could relieve himself. While doing so, Abbott worried that Adan was going to attack him or have him arrested for disorderly or threatening conduct since, inside, he had raised his voice when Adan refused to let him use the employee bathroom. He also worried about what the two young ladies sitting at one of the tables inside were thinking. One was a student at Barnard and a native of the Philippines and the other a resident of France, who had accompanied him to the café after a night of dancing. Later, Abbott claimed Adan had a knife. Abbott definitely had a knife. Emerging from behind the Dumpster, he again confronted Adan, his anger at being refused use of the facilities in front of his female guests still smoldering. This time, the soft-spoken night manager tried to diffuse the situation by turning his back on Abbott while inviting him to return to the restaurant. Suddenly, Abbott pulled out a four-inch blade, grabbed his victim from behind, and plunged the knife into his chest, nearly slicing Adan's heart in half. Abbott ran back into the restaurant and announced that he had just killed a man and had to flee. The young women fled, too, but they didn't leave the area; instead, they stood a block away looking back at the scene of the attack until somebody identified them to police as appearing to have knowledge about the crime and they were brought back for questioning. Adan lay dead on the littered pavement. Abbott would soon be on his way to Mexico.

Thus began and ended the brief and fleeting literary career of Jack Henry Abbott, even though he would write another book a few years later. That morning also changed forever the way Norman

Mailer would view the artist or the writer as outlier, an idea he had asserted in the controversial essay "The White Negro" in 1959. Literary talent might not, should not, trump personal conduct—the man who had once stabbed his wife, nearly killing her, would conclude. Mailer had been one of the principal agents of Jack's release from prison. He had promised to employ the ex-con as a literary assistant, and he had written an introduction to *In the Belly of the Beast*. The book consisted of prison letters Abbott had written to Mailer while he worked away on *The Executioner's Song*, his magnum opus and the work that would win him his second Pulitzer Prize, in 1980. Without those letters from Abbott, who told him what it was truly like to grow up behind bars, as Gary Gilmore, the focus of *The Executioner's Song,* had essentially done, Mailer said he could not have written the book he did. "Your letters," he told Abbott as he was finishing his work, "have lit up corners of the book for me that I might otherwise not have comprehended or seen only in the gloom of my instinct unfortified by experience. Often the things you say corroborate my deepest instincts about what prison must be like."[1] Although he had spent brief time in city jails and seventeen days in Bellevue Hospital following the stabbing of his second wife in 1960, Mailer had never been in prison. Abbott and Gary Gilmore were incarcerated in the same prison at the same time—two, in fact: the Utah State Prison in Draper and the United States Penitentiary in Marion, Illinois.

"When you got down to it," Mailer wrote in the introduction to Jack's book, "I did not know much about violence in prison." He read carefully Abbott's letters describing it, which Mailer wrote, "did not encourage sweet dreams." Unlike Gilmore's description of prison in his letters to his girlfriend, Abbott's were not romantic. Abbott "was not interested in the particular," as Gilmore was, but only in the relevance of those particulars "to the abstract. Prison, whatever its nightmares, was not a dream whose roots would lead you to eternity, but an infernal machine of destruction, a design for the Dispose-All anus of a prodigiously diseased society."[2]

This is the story of the author and the apprentice. It is the story of literary influence and tragedy. It is the story of a state-raised convict, the "by-blow," as Melville says of another of society's orphans in *Billy Budd,* a novel that comes into play in our story; of an army drunk; and a Eurasian prostitute. It is the story of a writer who set out all his life to write the Great American Novel and stumbled into its greatness as essentially a gifted journalist whose "true life novel" transcends the quotidian world of facts. Finally, it is the story of incarceration in America.

JACK and NORMAN

1

Gilmore in the Flesh

Norman Mailer was less than halfway through a first draft of *The Executioner's Song*, a book of just over a thousand pages, when he heard from Federal Prisoner 87098-132. "Violence in America: A Novel in the Life of Gary Gilmore" was then the working title for what would arguably become Mailer's magnum opus. As in the case of his book on Marilyn Monroe in 1973, the author got the basis of his story from Lawrence Schiller, a photographer for *Life* magazine and a media entrepreneur. Schiller had purchased the rights to the Gilmore story. The convicted double murderer was executed by a Utah firing squad on January 17, 1977. It was the first use of capital punishment in the United States since 1973, when the Supreme Court had ruled the death penalty as it was then practiced cruel and unusual punishment, in part because of a lack of uniform criteria. The states, especially Texas, where Gilmore was born, quickly rectified the problem, and the high court approved the changes in 1976. Yet even Texas, which has easily led the field in executions since their resumption, took another six years to execute somebody. No one state, certainly not Utah, apparently wished to be the first to resume the death penalty in America. When Gilmore insisted that his sentence be carried out on schedule, bypassing the normal appeal process, he became a household name, his "death wish" sounded around the world, his picture splashed on the cover of *Newsweek* and most tabloids. He was quoted as telling the judge who had delivered the death judgment: "You sentenced me to die. Unless it's a joke or something, I want to go ahead and do it."

Hardly a year later, on February 9, 1978, Gary Gilmore's "ghost" wrote to Norman Mailer. His name was Jack Henry Abbott. Like Gilmore, Abbott had been practically "born" into prison, grown into adulthood as a "state-raised convict." His earliest memories, he said, were that of a string of foster homes he had run away from. Gilmore, on the other hand, had come from an intact, if also dysfunctional, family. After repeated run-ins with the law, he had entered the adult prison system as a habitual criminal, at about the same age that Abbott had entered adult prison, after graduating from six years of reform school and experiencing only seven months of freedom. In age Gilmore and Abbott were only four years apart—Gilmore was born on December 4, 1940; Abbott, on January 21, 1944. Both became career convicts.

Abbott had read "somewhere" that Mailer was working on the Gilmore saga, still sizzling in the public memory since the sensational execution in which the condemned prisoner's last words to the prison warden were allegedly, "Let's do it." Abbott claimed that he had known Gilmore at Utah State Prison—had even cared for or written to the same girl from prison—and considered him a "good convict," a man of honor who was respected in prison because he was feared in prison. Abbott had been in prison long enough to know its evil firsthand. "Only after fifteen years in prison," he told Mailer, "does one begin to see what is happening to us." He urged him not to listen to anybody who had been in and out of prison for twenty years. That kind of convict knew nothing, he said. Neither did "those sheltered ghetto shit talkers" who would die of fright when confronted with the violence he had faced. "I can tell you stories and help you. I'd like to."[1]

Abbott was thirty-four when he first wrote to Mailer from the federal prison in Butner, North Carolina, where he was being held temporarily. He had begun his adult imprisonment in 1963, in the Utah State Prison in Draper, where Gilmore had also been confined—and executed. Convicted at the age of eighteen of forging checks worth more than $20,000 from an establishment he had burglarized, Abbott was initially sentenced to a maximum of five years; his time was extended to a term of three to twenty years for killing an inmate and assaulting another. That was in 1966. Five years later, in 1971, he escaped from Draper, possibly the first prisoner to do so, and remained a fugitive for six weeks. He was apprehended after holding up a bank in Denver for the "express purpose," he told Mailer, of getting into the federal prison system. For this crime, he was sentenced to a term of nineteen years, after which he was to be returned to Utah to complete his twenty-year sentence. Of his last twenty years of incarceration, including the first six at the Utah State Industrial School for Boys, he had been "free" only seven months.

During his confinement at Draper, he claimed to have spent

more than five years in solitary confinement. According to Warden Sam Smith, "The majority of [Abbott's] time in prison [there] was spent in segregation and Maximum Security because of numerous and repeated disciplinary reports." Even so, Abbott was given a parole hearing for May 1966, "provided he held a clean institutional record"—which he did not maintain. Between 1966 and 1971, when he escaped with another inmate, Abbott had received thirty incident and disciplinary reports, including the assault of two prison guards.[2] When Mailer read this report, on the eve of Abbott's release in 1981, he naively scoffed at "friend Smith" calling Abbott "a management problem." Despite clear evidence in Abbott's letters to the contrary, the author of *The Executioner's Song* was willing to bet that Abbott was no longer violent or a danger to society.

Some think Abbott was simply good at conning his middle-class friends. Jerzy Kosinski, probably best known for the dramatization of his novel *Being There,* evidently thought so. He and Abbott had corresponded in the early seventies, when Kosinski was president of the American chapter of PEN and involved in the "prison movement." As president of PEN, he had reactivated its prisoners' program, in which books were sent to prisoners, who were encouraged to enter writing contests in the various genres. Abbott submitted fiction, but it was surely based on the hard facts of a lifetime in prison. "He wrote his first letter to me in 1973," Kosinski told an interviewer, "because he had read *The Painted Bird*; and because in the novel the boy is saved by the Red Army, Abbott assumed . . . I was, like him, a Soviet sympathizer." This misunderstanding eventually led to an unpleasant parting of the ways in which Abbott, a Marxist-Leninist and a pro-Stalinist, accused Kosinski of using without permission ideas from some of his letters in the novel *Cockpit* (1975). "Abbott," Kosinski complained, "embarked on the most sustained, vile barrage of personal, sexual, political, and aesthetic abuse, dissecting my novels and filtering them through his notion of my betrayal of mankind . . ." (Later, Abbott tried to make amends, but Kosinski had had enough and answered no more of his letters. "I didn't reply, and he abandoned me as a potential rescue system." He waited, Kosinski added, until he came upon Mailer, hoping he would be more receptive than Kosinski to his boiling sense of outrage.)[3]

As Abbott would write in *In the Belly of the Beast* (1981), as a sixth-grade dropout, his formal schooling consisted almost solely of reading in prison. By 1978, he had become a communist and was running informal prison seminars on Marxism. He was steeped in the works of many other philosophers, works by Kierkegaard, Nietzsche, and Sartre, for example. "Over the years," he wrote in his blockbuster book, "my sister had books sent to me from a single bookstore, and the people who owned it searched out titles they did not have in stock, free of extra charge, to send to me."[4] Ninety percent of his vocabulary he had never heard spoken by the time he wrote to Mailer. His IQ, he noted, was 138 (for whatever that's worth today, Mailer's was supposedly 170), and Abbott claimed that he had spent his life as a "good convict"—that is, not an obedient inmate but one who never "snitched," an assertion that would ultimately be challenged.

Initially famous for *The Naked and the Dead*, published in 1948 and widely considered the best novel to come out of World War II, Mailer spent the next thirty years trying to return to the same literary heights. Although his name hadn't ever been altogether out of the limelight, or the journalistic headlights, for that matter, it also hadn't—because of his outsized public personality—been there entirely for his bestselling fiction or even for the fact that he won his first Pulitzer for *The Armies of the Night* in 1969. Dependent solely on his writings and beset by alimony and child support payments, as he went from wife to wife, he wrote too fast. His career pattern bore an uncanny resemblance to that of one of his literary heroes, Theodore Dreiser. Like Dreiser, who first became famous with *Sister Carrie* in 1900 and again with *An American Tragedy* in 1925, Mailer would begin and essentially end his literary career with masterpieces. Indeed, if Dreiser is, as he is known, the "Father of American Realism," Mailer became his literary son with his pair of deterministic novels. As an undergraduate at Harvard, Mailer had taken a seminar taught by the renowned scholar Howard Mumford Jones that focused on Dreiser and William Faulkner. It was a new connection even for the late 1940s, long before we came to see clearly the psychological underpinnings of *An American Tragedy*, which Mailer would use as his model for telling the story of Gary Gilmore. Mailer was intimately familiar with both of Dreiser's masterpieces, if not his entire oeuvre.

In *Marilyn* he had suggested a parallel between Carrie Meeber and Marilyn Monroe, each a *jeune fille* in the urban jungle of America. While on the West Coast as a hopeful screenwriter, an experience that provided the basis for *The Deer Park* (1955), Mailer tutored Shelley Winters on the role of Roberta Alden, the factory girl seduced and murdered in *An American Tragedy*, help that convinced director George Stevens to give her the part in *A Place in the Sun* (1951), a dramatization of the novel. Roberta, Mailer told Winters, is "a girl completely without artifice." So was Carrie in the beginning of *Sister Carrie*, the girl next door, or kid sister, before she found her footing in Chicago and New York.[5]

Sister Carrie had come right out of Dreiser's tattered youth and peripatetic family, whereas *An American Tragedy* had come from the newspapers. The first had been fiction; the second had been "fact," or creative nonfiction. Dreiser's books in between never quite made it as American classics, at least not in the way *Sister Carrie* and *An American Tragedy* did. The same became true for Mailer, whose fictional work between *The Naked and the Dead* and *The Executioner's Song* had the same kind of belabored plots as Dreiser's middle works. In both cases, the dialogue had a tinny sound to it, and the plots were somewhat overwrought, as if an argument rather than a theme were at the heart of the works. In *Barbary Shore* (1951), for example, whatever plot Mailer envisioned for his second novel evaporates into a political argument about the dangers of post–World War II fascism.

Both writers required a flesh-and-blood protagonist to relocate themselves in their writing lives. Mailer's turning point from fiction to fact, or creative nonfiction, probably came first with *The Armies of the Night* (1968), for which he won not only the Pulitzer but also the National Book Award. Having taken part in the 1967 march on the Pentagon to protest the Vietnam War, he married in his narrative the historical and the fictional to drive one of the first nails into the coffin of a war that was unwinnable. This nonfiction pattern was continued elsewhere, most notably in *The Fight* (1975). In fact, one of the chapter titles in this short work is called "The Executioner's Song." It applies to Muhammad Ali's destruction of heavyweight George Foreman in the "Rumble in the Jungle" in 1974. Mailer had been ringside to cover the fight for *Playboy*, but the story he subsequently wrote about the former Belgian Congo became something more than journalism. In modern-day Zaire he found in Ali the "psychic outlaw" he had envisioned in "The White Negro" (1957), somebody who would strike back at society for its hypocrisies. The prison movement of the early 1970s may have fueled his fascination with such a hero, though the figure appears in earlier fiction, indeed as early as Lieutenant Hearn in *The Naked and the Dead*.

From the very beginning, Jack Abbott was clearly looking for another "potential rescue system." Doubtless, Mailer saw that, but he was nevertheless drawn into Abbott's world. It was a journey deep into the dungeons of the nation's incarcerated, an exploration Mailer needed for his book. Yet he was also smitten by Abbott's prose style. The convict had his own "voice." Hence, as the apprentice sought to acquire Mailer's support for his first parole hearing in the federal system, which he thought might take place as early as 1982, he not only educated the author but also intrigued and infatuated him. His problem, he told Mailer, was that as a state prisoner in Utah, he had been labeled one of the "most dangerous." Now in the federal system, he was having the same problem. Just the year before, he had been found "guilty" of tying up a guard and stabbing him. Yet for some reason he was indicted only for striking a prison doctor who was trying to "zonk" him with Thorazine.

Saying that he couldn't write ("wish I could!"), he proceeded to astonish Mailer with stories of overpowering detail, drama, and irony. He offered the novelist access to his state and federal files as long as it was merely for the purpose of comprehending prison, saying that Mailer would never get another chance to obtain material as valuable as he was offering him. "Frankly," he said, "there is no prisoner who has been involved in so much in-fighting at prison as myself who is still alive." There wasn't, he added, a single federal penitentiary that would willingly accept him as a permanent transfer. Only somebody like Jack Henry Abbott, Mailer soon came to realize, could get the author inside the head of Gary Mark Gilmore; only he could approximate the condemned man's inner rage and paranoia brought on by a lifetime behind bars. Abbott signed off in this first letter of February 9, 1978, as he would throughout their long correspondence, even after he had been let out and killed again—"In Peace, Jack."

Mailer responded to Jack's first letter almost immediately. It had been delivered through a third party, the literary agent Morton Janklow, so he probably didn't read it for a week or more. On February 23, 1978, he wrote Abbott that he was in the middle of the book and had only six months to "get the writing done before I'm dead broke." His advance was "half of a half million," but he had fourteen people to support. That meant, he later added, that he needed to make at least that much money every year. He was now married to his sixth wife, Norris Church, who had just given him his eighth child, John Buffalo Mailer, born April 16, 1978.

What he was trying to write in *The Executioner's Song* was a "factual" novel. He would soon realize from Abbott's letters that Gilmore's seeming twin hit powerfully on the psychology of violence in prison: "There are parts of this book," he told Abbott, "that I don't pretend to understand and prison life is a big part of it."[6] He sought to capture and dramatize the psychology of violence in prison. Abbott's very first letter convinced Mailer that he had much to learn about prison. Yet he wondered just where they would start. They had little more than six months to correspond before his publisher's deadline. He was also slightly edgy about Abbott, saying that he hadn't quite "understood" the prisoner's reference to "sheltered ghetto shit-talkers who would die of fright if confronted with real violence." Abbott would approach the same racism in *In the Belly of the Beast*, which came only in part from the original prison letters he would send Mailer. "How would you like to be forced all the days of your life," he wrote, "to sit beside a stinking, stupid wino every morning for breakfast? Or for some loud fool in his infinite ignorance to be at any moment able to say (slur) 'Gimme a cigarette, man.' "[7] In his letter to Mailer of October 8, 1978, the fool is a "loud nigger." Also left out of the book: "And I just look into his sleazy eyes and want to kill his ass there in front of god and everyone because it's not [that] he is black but that anyone with sense knows if he is not my friend he doesn't dare hit on me for anything."

2

Partners in Crime

On January 10, 1966, at age twenty-one, Abbott fatally knifed James L. Christensen and seriously wounded another inmate at the Utah State Prison in Draper. He later described the killing to Mailer as "prison combat."[1] There were few fistfights in prison. The risk of revenge was too great because you had to live in the same place as your enemy; there was no chance of moving away to avoid conflict. According to Abbott, enemies in Draper had followed him there from reform school. They allegedly egged on Christensen to "hit on" Abbott—to make him a prison wife. Knowing that this man was about to rape him as soon as he was released from the "hole," Abbott armed himself with a knife borrowed from an older con. When Christensen and his accomplice began to assault him with a club of some sort, Abbott stabbed Christensen so many times that he nearly severed his right arm from his body. The other assassin sustained a serious neck wound. Christensen died in the prison infirmary ten days later. After the fight, guards beat Abbott severely and sent him to solitary confinement for almost a month.[2]

Abbott was convicted on April 17, 1967, of assault with a deadly weapon, for the death of Christensen. Abbott's motive, it was stated, had in fact not been self-defense but simply revenge on Christensen for revealing to guards that Abbott possessed contraband in his cell. With good behavior, he could have been paroled in another fifteen years. But Abbott soon extended his time by breaking prison rules. He claimed he spent approximately half the years between 1967 and 1971, when he escaped, in solitary. In speaking of the six weeks he spent on the outside, which ended when he robbed a bank in Denver on April 27, 1971, Abbott recalled to Mailer the mixture of fear and euphoria of being free, really for the first time since he had been a teenager. His moving description of living "in the free world" was repeated almost verbatim in his book:

> I was in a hotel room in Montreal, Canada. I was asleep. I had been a fugitive for about three weeks. I began waking in the night in a sweat from bad dreams. I had simply been dreaming of prison . . . I had *forgotten* I was free, I had escaped. I could not grasp where I was. I was in a nice bedroom with fancy furnishings. A window was open and the sunlight was shining in. There were no bars. The walls were papered in rich designs. My bed was large and comfortable. So much more. I must have sat there in bed reeling from shock and numbness for an hour while it all gradually came back to me that I had escaped.[3]

With a twenty-year sentence in federal prison, Abbott would have been lucky even simply to dream about being free. Instead, he threw himself into reading whatever he could. He told Mailer that he had started reading at reform school, though some of the titles he names make it rather unlikely that he was reading so seriously so early.

When Mailer agreed to correspond with Abbott in 1978, he knew that Jack had stabbed somebody. Yet Mailer too had stabbed somebody, in 1960. Whether this uneasy parallel gave Mailer pause or discomfort is unknown, but his interest in learning more about prison life as he worked away on *The Executioner's Song* probably dashed any hesitation he may have felt about corresponding with Abbott. Mailer had stabbed his second wife with a two-and-a-half-inch penknife. The assault had taken place when he was about to make his first run for mayor of New York City. His political coming-out party on November 19 devolved into a drunken brawl. By four o'clock in the morning, when everyone had finally departed, Mailer, high on booze and marijuana, stabbed Adele Morales, whom he had married in 1954. Also heavily intoxicated, she had apparently called the Hemingwayesque writer a "queer." In fact, he stabbed her not once but twice—first in the stomach and again in the back. One of the wounds nearly pierced her heart.

How close Norman Mailer came to leading the life of Jack Abbott or Gary Gilmore. If Adele had pressed charges, he could have been sentenced to as many as twenty years in prison. If she had died, they could have thrown away the key. But Norman Mailer had not been born for jail. Despite growing up in a rough neighborhood, Mailer was fully middle-class, a graduate of Harvard, and the author of a bestselling novel. Instead of jail, Mailer was involuntarily committed to Bellevue Hospital for seventeen days and ultimately given a suspended sentence and three years' probation, after pleading guilty to a reduced charge of assault. Before his arrest, he had managed to sneak into Adele's hospital room and persuade her not to press charges. Their initial story was that Adele had fallen on some glass, but Mailer subsequently pled guilty to stabbing his wife. Only somebody who was somebody could have reasonably hoped to escape a prison sentence. Neither Gilmore nor Abbott ever had that chance in life.

Norman Kingsley Mailer was born on January 31, 1923, to Barney Mailer and Fanny Schneider in Long Branch, New Jersey. Of Lithuanian-Jewish descent, Barney had emigrated through England from South Africa, where he had been in the army during World War I. The British accent we sometimes heard in Norman Mailer's speech found its source in his father's South African dialect. Otherwise, the father was anything but the alpha male his son would grow up to become. A "natty" dresser who regularly ran up gambling debts, Barney had married Fanny the year before, and Norman was the first of their two children. His sister, Barbara, was born in 1927. Barney had been an accountant in South Africa, and he took up the same profession in the United States, where he had moved originally to visit his sister and her husband, David Kessler.

Fanny was the daughter of a part-time, unpaid rabbi in Long Branch, who had emigrated from Russia. Her family owned a grocery store. Apparently, Norman got his hyperactive temperament as well as his literary talent mostly from his mother and maternal grandfather. Mailer could also have inherited his grandfather's excitable nature. Rabbi Schneider could "flare up" on occasion.[4] Fanny and Barney lived in the Flatbush section of Brooklyn until Norman was nine, when the couple moved to the lower-middle-class Jewish community of Crown Heights. Barney was a loving but distant father, something Norman emulated as he became, time after time, marriage after marriage, the "quality time" father of eight children. He got his fire from his mother, who commandeered the household. This grandson of a rabbi went through bar mitzvah, but as an adult he joined the growing segment of Jews after World War II who were largely secularized. As a student, he was recognized for his exceptional intelligence. And unlike either Gary Gilmore or Jack Abbott, both of whom had specific talents (Gilmore in graphic arts, Abbott in writing), Mailer had an enviable environment in which to develop.

He entered Harvard at the age of sixteen. There, he met and eventually, in 1944, married Beatrice Silverman, a student at Boston University and—with the exception of the twenty-four-hour marriage to Carol Stevens in 1980, a longstanding mistress who had given him his seventh child—the only Jewish woman he ever married. They were married until 1952 and had one child, Susan, before they divorced. While Norman was in basic training as an enlisted man at an army camp in the South, in preparation for his military service in the Pacific in 1944, Beatrice joined the Navy WAVES and became an ensign, or commissioned officer, stationed in Washington, D.C. Known throughout his public life for his philandering and multiple marriages, Mailer, before he became famous at twenty-five as the author of *The Naked and the Dead*, apparently began his first marriage with the middle-class notion of maintaining a monogamous relationship. He wrote Bea from Fort Bragg in 1944 that it was "a funny thing [that] other men's sexual mores [were] so different from mine." When he told his army friends that he had been married only three months, they teased him incessantly, saying that most of them had enjoyed regular one-night stands before they were married.[5] Later on, especially after the publication of *The Naked and the Dead* in 1948, Mailer began the extramarital flings, many of which turned into marriages.

Mailer's second wife, Adele, was an artist who may have in some way wanted to "compete" with her husband the writer. On the night of the stabbing, one of the party guests thought she remembered Adele telling Mailer that he wasn't as good a writer as Dostoyevsky. Almost from the beginning, the marriage had become increasingly turbulent, much more so than his first marriage. Adele, who did not press charges against her husband, said that her primary reason was not Norman but her two children with him, Danielle and Elizabeth. She didn't want the story of the stabbing to get into the newspapers, which of course it did. Jean Malaquais, a Marxist-Leninist who first met Mailer in Paris and who had deeply influenced him early in his career as a writer (Malaquais would later, through Mailer, become a confidant of Abbott's), read about the incident in Paris and telegrammed Norman to say he was one hundred percent behind him. "Of course I was aware of his drinking and pills and marijuana," he told

Peter Manso. "He'd tried to smoke pot too, just as he was always trying to make me drink."[6]

At his lowest ebb professionally, if not personally, in the wake of the many damning reviews of *The Deer Park* (1955) and the audacity of *Advertisements for Myself* in 1959, Mailer began ever so slowly to turn away from pure fiction in the form of the novel and devote his writing genius to original forays into journalism and nonfiction. There would be several long magazine pieces, much work in *The Village Voice*, which he cofounded, and more novels, including *An American Dream* (1965), in which the narrator gets away with murder, but the Vietnam War and *The Armies of the Night* (1968) lay securely in his future as a writer of nonfiction. As J. Michael Lennon observes in Mailer's biography, "For the remainder of his career, he would move . . . from the novel to the essay, newspaper and magazine columns to poetry, plays to biography."[7]

Mailer had participated in America's last "good war." Not since the Civil War was the country so changed by such an event. The War of 1898 was brief, except for the U.S. experiment in imperialism that followed in the Philippines. And America came late into the Great War. One of the judges for the National Book Award in 1968, the literary historian Alfred Kazin, compared Mailer's treatment of the Vietnam War with Walt Whitman's autobiographical observations on the Civil War. Kazin believed *The Armies of the Night* to be "just as brilliant a personal testimony as Whitman's diary of the Civil War, 'Specimen Days,' and Whitman's great essay on the crisis of the Republic during the Gilded Age,

'Democratic Vistas.' " Mailer's book, Kazin noted, is "a work of personal and political reportage that brings to the inner and developing crisis of the United States at this moment admirable sensibilities, candid intelligence, the most moving concern for America itself. Mailer's intuition in this book is that the times demand a new form. He has found it."

Within a mere decade of having stabbed his wife and being confined in Bellevue, Mailer had returned not as a novelist but as a nonfiction writer who used the novelist's gifts to investigate the state of the American psyche.

It was Mailer's professional feeling, Kazin concluded, that the American scene in 1967 was "too thorny a subject to be left to journalists."[8] With *The Armies of the Night*, Mailer turned the corner of fiction for art's sake, so to speak. The same challenge lay ahead with *The Executioner's Song*, which he subtitled "a true life novel." Where its nonfiction might have run a little dry, the impact of Abbott's impassioned letters helped fill in the important emotional gaps. Actually, Mailer briefly considered placing some of Jack's letters "directly into the book, even incorporating some of [his] experience into Gilmore. But I came to the conclusion that I wanted nothing imaginary in Gilmore's makeup."[9] He ended up by merely thanking him extensively in the acknowledgments. And when the book came out, he was very anxious to learn what Abbott thought of the "novel." For in this novel, the factual truth was lifted up by the writer's imagination to reveal its full significance.

Like Gilmore, Abbott was not, he told Mailer on November 1, 1978, meant to serve a life term in prison. Both prisoners so hated it that they had to be subdued with Prolixen. He told of talking with another convict who saw Gilmore transfixed by the drug, a strong tranquilizer that leaves the recipient in a confused state for weeks afterward. Abbott realized, he said, that he had "made an identity with Gilmore," but he assured Mailer that there were many men like him, men, he said, who had entered the prison world "whole and healthy," only to be "soiled" by its endless repression and repetition. His mind, Abbott continued in a letter of November 17, 1978, kept turning on one of the principal aspects of prison "that separate prisoners who, at some point in their lives serve a few good years and get out never to return again" and convicts like himself and Gilmore who literally grow up in prison. Admitting to some mental instability, he blamed it on his "lifetime of penal incarceration" during which the convict develops a permanent case of "arrested adolescence." He wasn't even allowed to own a photograph of himself. While those whose stretches in prison are broken up by time in the "free world" often grow out of such adolescence to become men, the "state-raised" convict remains a child and is treated like one. At age thirty-four, Abbott confessed, "I am barely a precocious child." The state-raised convict's conception of manhood, he said, is gauged only by a capacity for revenge—or murder, the only avenue of effective revenge in prison. There, he concluded, "any pig can, and constantly *does* interfere with your affairs—no matter how innocent those affairs are and no matter how personal. You are not 'sir' or 'Mr. Mailer.' They (the pigs) are.

You are 'Mailer' or 'Norman' or, if they want to, you are any nickname they want to call you by."

Jack Henry Abbott would convey to the future author of *The Executioner's Song,* through his long letters, one of them fifty-eight handwritten pages, the bottomless desire for freedom, no matter how long or indefinite the prison sentence. Abbott helped to flesh out material on Gilmore provided by Larry Schiller and Gilmore's girlfriend, Nicole Baker Barrett. The long-term prisoner never gave up the hope of becoming free again. If he did, suicide was the only alternative. Abbott taught Mailer that even when Gilmore insisted on the state's carrying out his death penalty, he was doing so only because it was the only way to be free. If he could have gotten out of jail alive, he would have done so. In fact, as Mailer illustrates in *The Executioner's Song*, Gilmore asks two different visitors on the early morning of his execution if they would exchange clothes with him so that he could slip out with the other visitors. Mailer ultimately understood Gilmore through his empathy with Abbott. That empathy, however, would have its costs. Both the author and the prisoner had once knifed somebody, and the one who went to jail would do it again.

3

Eastern State Penitentiary

The Quakers in Pennsylvania opened Eastern State Penitentiary in 1829. The practice of incarceration, or long-term confinements, was new in America and had begun in Europe only in the eighteenth century. Before that, aside from fines, punishment consisted of banning, branding, maiming, the lash, or time in the public stocks. Generally, the only other punishment was death. Eastern State was not the first of what today penal reformers call America's "prison-industrial complex." The first such prison was built in Pittsburgh. It was demoted to a halfway house for drug addicts in 2007. Eastern State stands today as a preserved ruin in the Museum District of Philadelphia, having been closed in 1971. In its heyday, it held such infamous criminals as Al Capone and Willie Sutton, and one lesser known—a white-collar criminal named Charles Yerkes, who became the model for Dreiser's Frank Cowperwood in *The Financier* (1912). Eastern State was not originally intended, however, for major criminals. It was designed mainly for first offenders, and it more or less invented the concept of solitary confinement—today supposedly reserved for the worst behavior in prison, the kind of incarceration Jack Abbott claimed he knew so well.

Back then, the goal of punishment, or penance, took a back seat to the nobler goal of penitence. And prisons in those times, incidentally, were reserved for whites only. Free blacks were sent to county and city jails, where the accommodations were (and are generally still) much inferior to those in penitentiaries or prisons. At Eastern State Penitentiary each prisoner was assigned to a large, eight-by-ten-foot single cell that opened in the back to a small courtyard within the prison grounds. Here he was allowed to grow some of his own food, since gardening was considered the standard form of exercise in the nineteenth century. During the period of his incarceration, ordinarily from two to four years, the prisoner never saw or spoke to another human being except a guard. Whenever he was moved from one place to another in the prison, a large hood was placed over his head and shoulders.

The prison itself resembles a gothic castle and must have been a gloomy sight to the entering inmate. William Styron, writing of another early American prison, could easily have been writing of Eastern State when he called it "uncompromisingly somber," noting that "its very appearance seems calculated to implant in the mind of the onlooker the idea of justice in its most retributive sense."[1] The dungeon's European façade features two towers connected by iron gates. The walls are thirty feet high and twelve feet thick at the base. They form a square of nearly ten acres. Within those walls lay a wagon-wheel structure of six spokes, or cell corridors. The center formed a panopticon from which a single guard could keep an eye on the entire prison. The cells were all on one level until the twentieth century, when the prison was converted to accommodate more than twice as many prisoners, and cell wings on a second story were added. By then, each cell held two or three inmates, and prisoners were no longer "solitary," unless they were sent to the "hole," by that time a smaller cell with no light reserved for those who persistently disobeyed prison rules.

Prisoners in the nineteenth century were effectively removed from the world in which they had sinned. They were allowed nothing to read except the Bible and a few religious tracts. Such exiles were there to contemplate and to learn to feel sorrow for having committed their offenses. Even their names were taken away: "This rule" the founding wardens wrote, "prevents one convict from learning the name of another, and prevents that humiliation which invariably pursues a man when liberated, if he is known to have been an inhabitant of a penitentiary." The first prisoner took the number one. He was an eighteen-year-old farmer who had stolen, among other minor items, a twenty-dollar watch. He was sentenced to two years' confinement.[2]

Having lobbied the Pennsylvania legislature for many years to construct such a prison, which became a model for hundreds throughout the world, Quakers held to the concept of the Inner Light, or God, who would come to them as they sat and waited passively. Similarly, they thought that the grim isolation and deprivation of their new penal institution would bring the same light to those who had fallen away from the straight and narrow—that they, too, would perceive the Inner Light in the long-extended darkness of their confinement. The Quaker leaders were idealists who believed that all men, made in God's image, could be reformed—through solitude and reflection. Men were invested with power over their fellow men, they held, only to the extent of the "self-preservation and good order of society." They could not ignore the fact that even "the vilest criminal" confined to a prison cell "was invested by the Deity with a living soul, and however guilty against society . . . has unalienable rights which cannot be infringed."[3]

For those of God's creatures who misbehaved, however, the Quaker way could be ghastly unpleasant. "Extra-judicial punishments," as they were called, started out with mild restraints, such as the deprivation of exercise or food. The dungeon was reserved for those who continued to resist the invitation to reform. The prisoner was locked up in total darkness, "with nothing but a blanket to cover him, and in some cases he [was] even deprived of that covering." He was forced to sleep on a damp floor, and his daily food consisted of eight ounces of bread and "some water." There was also ducking, or "water-boarding," in which the offending prisoner was stripped naked and suspended by the wrists and drenched with water. In winter, icicles formed on the victim's hair and body. Worse yet was the "Mad, or Tranquillizing Chair" in which the prisoner was placed with his arms above the elbows fastened to the back of his chair: "A strap was passed round his body, through holes in the chair . . . His hands were linked together by hand cuffs. Straps were passed round the ankles and firmly fastened to the lower part of the chair. He had no resting place for his feet, there being no footboard. It was impossible for an individual thus manacled to move any part of his body or limbs."

Even more draconian was the application of the "iron gag." This rough instrument was forced into the prisoner's mouth; the iron pallet was placed over his tongue with "the bit forced in as far as possible, the chains brought round the jaws to the back of the neck." The inmate was cuffed with his hands behind him, and a chain connected the gag to the handcuffs. If the victim resisted by pulling his arms, the iron gag was forced deeper into his mouth—"the pressure consequently acting on the chains which press on the jaws and jugular veins, producing excruciating pain."[4]

Among those who visited Eastern State Penitentiary over the years, some examined the facility as an example of what they might construct back home, but others came for more humane reasons. One was Alexis de Tocqueville; another was Charles Dickens. Tocqueville, the author of the otherwise prescient *Democracy in America* (1835), visited the prison site in 1831 and was favorably impressed with the idea that the criminal was subjected to complete solitude: "Placed alone, in view of his crime, he learns to hate it . . . It is solitude, where remorse will come to assail him." Dickens, on the other hand, simply saw more of the misery he had recorded in his novels. After his 1842 visit to America and to Eastern State, he said in *American Notes*, published the same year, in a chapter entitled "Philadelphia and Its Solitary Prison," that he thought it to be "cruel and wrong." The intention of its founders, he wrote, was "kind, humane, and meant for reformation," but he was persuaded that "those benevolent gentlemen" obviously didn't realize that their "daily tampering with the mysteries of the brain [was] immeasurably worse than any torture of the body."[5] Victims of the iron gag would have disagreed.

"Standing at [the panopticon], and looking down these dreary passages," Dickens continued, "the dull repose and quiet that prevails, is awful. Occasionally, there is a drowsy sound from some lone weaver's shuttle, or shoemaker's last, but it is stifled by the thick walls and heavy dungeon-door, and only serves to make the general stillness more profound. Over the head and face of every prisoner who comes into this melancholy house, a black hood is drawn; and in this dark shroud, an emblem of the curtain dropped between him and the living world, he is led to the cell from which he never again comes forth, until his whole term of imprisonment has expired. He never hears of wife and children; home or friends; the life or death of any single creature. He sees the prison-officers, but with that exception he never looks upon a human countenance, or hears a human voice. He is a man buried alive; to be dug out in the slow round of years; and in the mean time dead to everything but torturing anxieties and horrible despair."[6]

By the turn of the twentieth century, Eastern State Penitentiary, like every other prison in the United States, was crowded and noisy—rife with brutality, incessant PA announcements, riots, hunger strikes, escapes, suicides, and scandals. The original goal of American "penitentiaries"—and eventually the entire concept of rehabilitation—was lost. The nineteenth-century practice of enforced penal solitude, so stifling and deadly, gave way to the din and profanity of men confined closely to one another. In the words of Michael Morton, who was wrongfully convicted of murder in 1987 and served twenty-five years in a Texas gulag, prisons today are " 'hate factories'—where inmates go in bad and come out worse, where men go in ashamed and come out angry."[7] The noise is nearly deafening. Today, even death row is as noisy as the general prison area. As Abbott wrote in his book, describing Marion, "You try to read, and find you've been reading the same paragraph for hours . . . You can't think or concentrate." In *An American Tragedy*, Theodore Dreiser described the hushed quiet of death row in Auburn Prison, where Chester Gillette, the real-life model for Clyde Griffiths, was executed in 1908. Back then, there was an enduring respect for life, even that of the convict about to go over to the other side. Guards wore slippers so as to move silently around the condemned.

Dreiser visited Eastern State in Philadelphia during the writing of his "true-life" novel, and Mailer may have as well during the composition of *The Executioner's Song*, or at least during one of his visits to lecture at the University of Pennsylvania, sponsored by his original authorized biographer, Professor Robert F. Lucid. It's hard to believe that the two didn't tour the old prison when Mailer was writing his book, if not earlier. In fact, in the mid-1950s, following the publication of *The Deer Park*, in which two of the principal characters serve time in jail, Mailer had wanted to write a book about prison, and even considered getting a job in a prison to learn of its horrors.[8] At Eastern State he would have seen at least the remains of such horrors—a crumbling memorial to the idea that man could be reformed, that through solitary confinement a prisoner might be made "penitent." The author and his original authorized biographer (who died in 2006 before writing his book) would have seen trees growing through the roofs of the building, crumbling prison cells, and rust everywhere. (During my own visit there in the summer of 1999, Roger Asselineau, a professor of American literature at the Sorbonne who had been sentenced to death by the Nazis, accompanied me. Following our tour of the prison ruin, he spoke quietly of his own incarceration and the concept of confinement in general—its claustrophobia and despair. At Eastern State, he readily entered one of its decaying cells, yet this veteran of the French Resistance became noticeably silent as he surveyed its darkness and decay. The Germans, he told me, had incarcerated him with two other prisoners in a small corner cell, or basement room, with only one window, high above their heads and partially blocked.) When Mailer took up the task of writing Gary Gilmore's story, he too entered a prison, not Eastern State but a virtual prison (enhanced by Abbott's letters) whose sordid surroundings and widespread despair reflected the failure of prisons to reform what society had already sealed off from itself.

"The founders of a new colony, whatever Utopia of human virtue and happiness they might originally project," Nathaniel

Hawthorne wrote in the opening of his masterpiece, *The Scarlet Letter* (1850), "have invariably recognized it among the earliest practical necessities to allot a portion of the virgin soil as a cemetery, and another portion as the site of a prison." (In the novel, Hester Prynne is confined in a prison used only to hold those who were to be exhibited in public, either on a scaffold or stocks.) In the chapter entitled "The Prison Door," he wrote, "The rust on the ponderous iron-work of its oaken door looked more antique than any thing else in the new world. Like all that pertains to crime, it seemed never to have known a youthful era." This historical novel about the Puritans, who were as idealistic as the Quakers of Philadelphia, is full of the same irony that haunts the American penal system, whose prisons are still called "penitentiaries."

"How I wish this would end! How I wish I could walk free in the world; could find my life again and see and do things other people do," Abbott wrote Mailer on September 24, 1978, well into their correspondence. "If society has the right to do to me what it has done (and is still doing), which society *does* have, then I have the right, at least, to at some time in my life walk free even if the odds are by now overwhelming that I may not be as other men; that I may, for example, do something like Gilmore did."[9] It was already too late for Abbott. He might not kill in cold blood like Gilmore, but he would kill to stay alive and retain his sense of dignity. He and Gilmore were hopelessly stuck in survival mode, or prison paranoia. To his dying day, Abbott would insist that when he killed a second time following his release in 1981, it was in self-defense, that his victim had a knife that subsequently got lost in the trash surrounding the street corner on which they fought. Although he conceded to Ed Bradley on *60 Minutes* (see chapter 16) that Adan might not have been armed, he continued after his conviction to ask friends "to search for Adan's knife in the alley."[10]

In a sense, Gary Gilmore may have killed to survive as well—he may have done so out of the same prison paranoia that overwhelmed Abbott. When he murdered a gas station attendant and a motel clerk, Gilmore was distraught because he had quarreled with his girlfriend, Nicole, and feared losing her. In *The Executioner's Song* we are told only that he killed because he feared losing Nicole after an argument, but Abbott suggested a different scenario after he had returned to prison and resumed his correspondence with Mailer. Abbott claimed that he had learned from a friend of his and Gilmore's that Gilmore actually had had a dispute over Nicole with his two victims ("This one's for Nicole," he is reported to have said as he put a second bullet into the head of the gas station clerk, in Mailer's version of events.) According to Abbott, who may have been simply trying to engage Mailer in continued correspondence after being sent back to prison, the gas station attendant had attempted to have sex with Nicole in recompense for money she owed on the repair of her car, and the motel clerk was gossiping that she had worked as a prostitute in his establishment, which, Abbott added, had been "a lie."[11]

The twentieth-century reality of releasing prisoners suffering from prison paranoia is a far cry from the utopian, reform-minded hopes of the Quakers who founded Eastern State. Yet in both cases prison tends to drive its victims "crazy" enough to kill. "The story of Jack Abbott," Peter Manso wrote of his interview with Abbott in 1982, did not "begin with the morning of Richard Adan's death, or even with Abbott's sudden celebrity [as the author of *In the Belly of the Beast*]. Indeed, as *The New York Times* editorialized at the conclusion of Abbott's trial, the killing of Adan as well as Jack Abbott's blasted hopes epitomized the 'awful failure of criminal justice.' "[12]

That system led Jack Abbott to hate the United States, to hate the rich who ran it for what they had done to him. He never felt any guilt over killing Richard Adan, merely remorse for the fact that it had happened. He had lost all feeling of guilt long before—in the series of foster homes he had run away from, in the Utah State Industrial School for Boys in Ogden, the Utah State Prison in Draper, and a series of federal lockups culminating with Marion, the meanest of them all and the prison that had replaced Alcatraz. But Jack had begun his prison odyssey at one of the worst, in Ogden, where punishments for what used to be called "juvenile delinquents" ranged from solitary confinement to whippings and the use of restraints. He is listed in a Wikipedia entry for the school as one of its two "Notable Internees." The other, coincidentally, also killed two people after his graduation from what was later renamed the Youth Development Center. Ronnie Lee Gardner (born in 1961) may have known Abbott when both were confined in Draper in 1980. He was executed by firing squad in 2010, like that other Mormon, Gary Gilmore, who chose that method over lethal injection because it involved the "blood atonement" adopted by the Church of the Latter-Day Saints in the nineteenth century (i.e., spilling blood for one's sins).

4

Marion Federal Prison

After being captured for robbing a Denver savings and loan during his flight from Draper in 1971, Abbott became a federal prisoner. Because of his disciplinary record, he rode the carousel of federal prisons during the next decade—Leavenworth, Lompoc, Atlanta, Springfield, Terminal Island, Lewisburg, Butner, and Marion. From La Tuna, the U.S. prison in the desert northeast of El Paso, halfway down a barren highway between there and Las Cruces, New Mexico, he told Mailer on September 22, 1978, "I'm surrounded by Mexican aliens here. No one speaks English, and I speak a little Spanish. They piss in the shower and refuse to flush toilet tissue down the toilet—you see heaps of shit-stained toilet tissue go past your cell in the wake of the trustee's push broom when he sweeps the corridor. Flies move in herds, like miniature cattle grazing a few feet above the floor." This remarkable description was included in *In the Belly of the Beast*. Perhaps to absolve himself of racial prejudice, he added, "In Mexico—as in most foreign countries—the water pressure in sewer plumbing is too low to accommodate the flushing of wet paper. This is why most of them who have never lived in this country—and speak no English—do not flush."

Abbott spent most of his federal time at the penitentiary in Marion, predecessor to what we now call "supermax" prisons. "We all know what Marion is," Abbott wrote from the federal Metropolitan Detention Center when he was headed back there following his conviction for killing Adan. "It was constructed strategically, in the dead-center of a geographical area legendary for being the homeland of lynchings, . . . legendary for the backwardness of its populace. It sits in the middle of a wood, surrounded by *miles* of bare flatland . . . The local radio stations broadcast 'talk shows' and the local rednecks—both the very young and the very old—telephone the radio stations and, their voices crackling over the air, go into *detail* regarding how they 'feel' inmates at Marion should be liquidated or 'put to use' in various (and inventive) new forms of slavery and experimental torture."[1]

In the 1990s Marion was downgraded to a medium-security prison. It was replaced by the federal prison in the middle of yet another nowhere—Fremont County, Colorado. ADX Florence, also known as "the Alcatraz of the Rockies," which specializes in solitary confinement and holds such prisoners as Ted Kaczynski, the "Unabomber," and Terry Nichols, the accomplice of Timothy McVeigh in the 1995 Oklahoma City bombing. Most of the prisoners at ADX Florence, as at Marion, are sent there because of their extensive disciplinary records, not because of their notoriety as criminals. This is why Jack Abbott was sent to Marion. After serving time at Marion, he was paroled in 1981, returning in the mid-1980s to serve the rest of his federal sentence. He was last released from Marion in 1986 and sent back to New York to serve a fifteen-year-to-life sentence for first-degree manslaughter.[2]

Abbott was in Marion, therefore, when the prison brought back the use of long-term solitary confinement, something that had been abandoned in the nineteenth century at Eastern State Penitentiary because it had so often led to insanity and death. Its wholesale return came about at Marion in 1983, but it was applied frequently enough before that time. Known after 1983 as the "Marion Lockdown," it was adopted following the murder of two prison guards. Marion and others like it became known as "control-unit" prisons, in which the inmate was often held in a windowless cell with a buzzing electric light over his head. Marion, like Eastern State Penitentiary before it, became a model for this method of incarceration, which attracted prison architects and directors from around the world. As Nancy Kurshan describes it, the application of the "hole" varied from prison to prison, "but generally speaking, a control-unit prison is one in which every prisoner is locked away in their own individual box about 23 hours a day under conditions of severe sensory deprivation—much in the way of Eastern State Penitentiary in the nineteenth century. The prisoner eats, sleeps and defecates in the windowless cell. Meals come through a slot in the door. In some cases the prisoner may be out of the cell a couple of times a week for exercise, but in other circumstances the exercise area is even more limited and is attached to the cell itself. Most control-unit prisons have little access to education or any recreational outlets."[3] Even outside the "hole," prisoners at Marion found themselves in what Abbott described to Mailer on July 31, 1979, as "the tightest prison in the world." There were more guards than prisoners, and prisoners went everywhere in the lockup in handcuffs and leg chains.

Before his release from prison in 1981, Abbott claimed to have served years in solitary confinement, not because of any general lockdown policy, but because of his repeated disciplinary infractions. One has to wonder, however, just how he found so much time to read all that he did. The only reading material generally available to prisoners in segregation was the Bible. In Utah the list extended to include, naturally, the Book of Mormon. "No other reading matter or religious matter allowed," he wrote in his book.[4] That Abbott may have exaggerated the total length of time he spent in solitary is evident simply from the reading knowledge he acquired in prison. He read rapaciously and continually beginning in the mid- to late 1960s, and when he wasn't reading, he was writing—long letters, often written with a pencil only two or three inches long so that it wouldn't constitute a weapon.

As his prison misconduct in the federal system continued and worsened, Abbott became known as a reformer among fellow inmates and troublemaker to his jailers. In making the rounds of the many federal prisons as a result, he landed for the first time, in 1979, at Marion. When, by 1980, he received a tentative parole date from federal authorities, he decided to break the inmate code he had so often boasted to Mailer about in his letters and became a "snitch." Around December 12, 1980, he identified the leaders of what became at the time the longest strike in federal prison history. Through biographer Peter Matthiessen, Mailer got wind of this information the following year, before it became public with the Adan stabbing, while Jack was still at a halfway house in New York. Although shocked that Jack had broken the inmate code he had all along boasted that he would uphold, Mailer let the matter go, wondering about what lengths he himself might go after half a lifetime in prison.

Before Abbott was released from Marion and sent back to Draper in June 1980, he provided Marion authorities with the names of the prisoners involved in arranging strikes and other offenses, such as plans to murder another convict or using illegal drugs. He testified that "progressive" attorneys for the Marion Prisoners' Rights Project were smuggling in drugs to inmates, otherwise misusing the prison mail system, and encouraging inmates to make false statements. As Abbott allegedly told Michael Hursey, an assistant U.S. district attorney for the Southern District of Illinois, and Richard Phillips, chief parole officer at Marion, "I had to think of my parole." With possibly only another eight months of prison to go, he couldn't stand the thought of losing this long-awaited chance for freedom. "I been down 19 years in January, and I just had to make the decision."[5]

Abbott later denied most of this story, hiding the fact of his willingness to do anything to become free, saying that before being sent back to Draper, he was told that in order to be granted federal parole he would have to "clear up" a few matters pertaining to the history of his imprisonment. For the next two months, he later testified, he was isolated from the prison population to give them the impression that he was busy "snitching." During this period, he "confessed," he said, to alleged crimes he had committed in prison in order to temper the accusations that would be made against guards in *In the Belly of the Beast*, when it was published in 1981.[6]

This is probably a good place to add an important note about Abbott's release, for which Mailer was almost singularly blamed after the Adan stabbing. Whether he snitched or not, Abbott probably would not have been let go without Mailer's influence as well as that of Robert Silvers, the editor who had read unpublished samples of Abbott's prison letters to Mailer and who would publish essays by Abbott in *The New York Review of Books*; Scott Meredith, Mailer's literary agent who also acted for Abbott; Erroll McDonald, Abbott's editor for *In the Belly of the Beast* at Random House—all of whom wrote letters on behalf of Abbott in an effort probably orchestrated by Mailer.[7] Moreover, in his pitch to the parole board, Mailer promised to employ Jack as his literary assistant. Proof of employment is always crucial in such cases; Gary Gilmore got out because he had a job in his uncle's shoe repair shop in Utah. Abbott's snitching may have clinched the deal.

After he "talked," Abbott feared for his life and insisted on protection from his fellow inmates. Betwixt and between, he didn't dare carry a concealed weapon because its discovery by guards would have ruined his chances for parole. Yet without a weapon he was vulnerable. He feared he would end his days in the prison graveyard. Even if armed, he couldn't "wait on the defensive because when it comes, it comes, and there's only one shot, and if somebody brings it to me to kill me, I got to bring it to them."[8] He described in his book just how he would "bring it to" someone with what he called "an intimate weapon":

> Here is how it is. You are both alone in [the attacker's] cell. You've slipped out a knife (eight- to ten-inch blade, double-edged). You're holding it beside your leg so he can't see it. The enemy is smiling and chattering away about something . . . You see the spot. It's a target between the second and third button on his shirt . . . A light pivot toward him with your right shoulder and the world turns upside down: you have sunk the knife to its hilt into the middle of his chest.[9]

Following his trial and conviction in 1982 for killing Richard Adan and his return to Marion to finish his original sentence, he rightfully feared that the inmates on whom he had squealed were waiting to get their revenge. Abbott survived his second stretch in Marion in a special section of the prison known as the Secure Unit. He also had the Marion guards to fear because many of them, he was positive, wanted revenge for what he had said about "pigs" in his book. So the new system of individual isolation may have saved him from the guards as well. Indeed, to get out of Marion the first time, he had claimed that he, along with six or seven other prisoners, had been brutally tortured on April 28, 1980—a lie he had to recant in order to get out of Marion after his first time there. Abbott had initially alleged that nine guards wearing masks and armed with clubs flogged his spine and made him beg for his life. This account of brutality was supposed to be part of *In the Belly of the Beast*, but Abbott withdrew it at the last opportunity. His Random House editors later told the press that its excision had been part of his agreement to get out of Marion.[10]

When Jack Abbott had first learned in 1980 that he would be paroled from the federal system in another year or so, he was nearly ecstatic—even though he faced the possibility of two or three more years back in Draper to finish his state sentence before a federal probation. "I *still* cannot comprehend that I am really going to be free in a few more years," he told Mailer. "Eighteen months left in the federal prison system and then the Utah prison once more . . . With a little help, a little luck, the Utah parole board will set me free after 2 more years. That will have given them 20 years of my life in a single stretch. A little over 3 years and I will, for the first time in my remembered life, be free; my own man." He couldn't, he said, comprehend his "good fortune." The prospect of freedom was frightening, not only because it would seem alien to him after so many years but also because he feared that his undiscovered and thus unpunished prison "sins of the past" would catch up with him and derail his parole.[11]

He was to be liberated for the first time in his "remembered life." Was it even possible that he could tolerate freedom after so many years of incarceration—years during which his hair-trigger temper was all he had had to protect him? Prisons, he said, create in prisoners a sense of necessary paranoia. Even the prison movement was ultimately false, or carried out under false pretenses, he thought: "[T]he radicals of the (so-called) New Left all came to us, particularly after Vietnam, to find something to sustain their anger, their rage."[12] Only Mailer, it seemed, could be trusted.

Around the time of his actual release, *The New York Review of Books* of June 11, 1981, published "Discovering Jack Abbott," the Mailer essay that became the basis of the introduction to *In the Belly of the Beast*. The *NYRB* had already published two items by Abbott. In the piece entitled "In Prison," published June 26, which is a selection of Abbott's letters Mailer had shown to editor Robert Silvers, Abbott wrote that he had been looking through steel bars for so long that "it's odd not to see bars everywhere." He noted that the knife—"the symbol of power on all prison yards"—was, like the bars, also steel. In a follow-up to "In Prison," published on October 9, which the *NYRB* entitled "Solitary Confinement," he spoke of the "alienating power of solitary confinement," which he said was "not constructed to complement human existence." He also primed the pump for his book by describing a strip cell. Being in one, he wrote:

> is identical to being in a sink. It is a square "room" with a hole in the center. The floor inclines like the bottom of a sink. The hole in the floor is the "toilet." It sits flush with the concrete floor . . . . There is nothing else in the room—except for a bare light bulb on the ceiling, well out of reach. The "toilet" is flushed by an apparatus outside the cell (at the guard's whim). There is no water facility nor even the semblance of a bed rack . . . . Nothing but the

smell of shit and piss and the glare of light that is never extinguished.

Jack was a known quantity before he got out of prison, a literary "find." On March 5, 1981, the *NYRB* had also published a review entitled "The Condemned," of a book about death row—Doug Magee's *Slow Coming Dark: Interviews on Death Row.* Abbott thought the title "exceedingly dramatic," saying that nobody in modern American times on death row actually expects to die. When it finally comes after years of appeals, its darkness is never slow, but "sudden; as sudden as an airplane careening out of control." He spoke, he said, from personal experience. He recalled his own temporary stay on death row in Utah, for three years, both before and after his prosecution for the killing of Christensen in 1966. ("They discussed executing me on local television," he wrote Mailer on December 15, 1978, "while my sister watched, frightened, while I lay chained to the floor in a strip-cell adjacent to death-row at age 21!") In his letter to Mailer, he penned a touching description of former death row prisoners as eccentrics who were both the most educated and the most vulnerable of all. All had served around twenty years under a death sentence when it was commuted to life in prison: "They lived in a different world from us—preferring the solitude of their cells to the crowded yard, staying in a recreation area where they carried on quiet pursuits, like stamp collecting, drawing, reading . . . I remember them as a fleeting species, forever slipping away to their cells."

Conjuring up the name of Gary Gilmore, whose death row story is the culmination of his own story, Abbott closed his *NYRB* review with the condemned man's plea that, "after all is said and done, that we are only human and it is not necessary to kill us. More than that none of us can offer: a life behind bars is enough."

In his introduction, Mailer wrote that Abbott and Gilmore had a lot in common. Both had been juvenile delinquents who were incarcerated for most of their adolescent years. As a result of their subsequent long sentences as adults, they were, "by their logic," part of the elite of the prison population. In his earliest letters to Mailer, Abbott had observed that their kind was fast disappearing from the prison populations across America. Whereas prison was equipped to "grind down criminals who are cowards," they could not break the spirit of those who see themselves as "men who set the code for this city-state, this prison." By the time Mailer began his correspondence with Abbott, he had become much less enamored of the Marxist-Leninist ideology that Abbott had acquired in prison than he was of Abbott's emerging literary gift. Abbott "had forged his revolutionary ideas out of the pain and damage done to his flesh and nerves by a life in prison," he wrote. It was very possible, Mailer continued, that Abbott would be just as much or more a revolutionary after a decade of freedom. "Or an altogether different kind of man." Whatever the case, he admired Jack Abbott "for surviving and for having learned to write as he does."[13]

5

Raised in a Box

Jack Abbott wrote two books in prison, not just the one he is known for. With the assistance of Naomi Zack, who married Abbott after he was sent back to prison following his trial for the slaying of Richard Adan, he wrote *My Return*, which was published in 1987. Discussion of it belongs to a later chapter of this book. What is worth mentioning here is its epigraph from Herman Melville's *Billy Budd*: "God bless Cap'n Vere!" These are the last words of the executed sailor whose death in the novella is likened to the Crucifixion. *Billy Budd* is the story of a young man convicted of killing the master-at-arms on a British warship at sea. You might want to say, "falsely accused," but Billy Budd in fact strikes Claggart dead in front of Captain Vere, who, because he fears mutiny from his crew, must prosecute the sailor to the letter of the law.

Billy, however, is only guilty according to the law of man, not God. He strikes the master-at-arms when accused falsely of mutinous conduct, but only because he cannot speak. Billy stutters. "Billy," Melville tells us, "was a striking instance that the arch interferer, the envious marplot of Eden, still has more or less to do with every human consignment to this planet of Earth." Instead of defending himself against Claggart's effort to frame him, Billy speaks with his fist. As a teenager and well into his incarcerated twenties, Jack Abbott also stuttered, and he attacked prison guards. He blamed his stutter on prison—that is, on the effect of waking up every day in a cell or, too often, in the bleakness of solitary confinement. He told Mailer that as a young man he suffered from claustrophobia and would fall into rages. At age thirty-six he still stuttered occasionally, when he had to address a guard—politely, that is. It was strange, he thought, that he could also cuss out a guard without the slightest hint of a stutter. He added, thinking possibly of Melville's stutterer, that people with such a defect "can usually sing without stuttering. Well, I can cuss without stuttering."[1] *My Return* was his extended attempt to defend himself for the paranoid stabbing of Richard Adan. The epigraph clearly summons forth his identification with Billy, who, "quick as the flame from a discharged cannon at night," drops Claggart to the deck.[2]

Melville subtitled his novella "An Inside Narrative" and set off the phrase even further with parentheses, as if to hide the fact that in his old age he may have been addressing his long dead mentor in the art or what he called "the power of blackness." Nathaniel Hawthorne is mentioned elsewhere by name in the story, written in the 1890s but not published until 1924, as "an honest scholar, my senior," who was then "no more." Back when *The Scarlet Letter* and *Moby-Dick* were published in 1850 and 1851, respectively, the two writers were neighbors and had debated whether evil originated from the head or the heart, the intellect or the emotions. In *Billy Budd* Melville sees the heart as the villain—that is, Claggart hates Billy because he is jealous of him, not because the sailor has ever wronged him. Jack Abbott's narrative is that he is as innocent as Billy Budd—guilty perhaps before the law but ultimately innocent because of what Melville calls "the marplot of Eden."

Jack Henry Abbott was the son of an Irish American from Texas and a Eurasian American from Utah. He was born on a military base in Oscoda, Michigan, during the final years of World War II. His parents were Mattie Jung, of Salt Lake City, and Rufus Henry Abbott, of Wichita Falls. Rufus was the third husband of the strikingly beautiful but headstrong Mattie. Both sides of Jack's family refused to recognize either him or his older half-sister, Frances, because of their mixed race. Mattie had six children in all, but she put the other four up for adoption. Rufus was an alcoholic who served in the Army Air Corps in the Pacific during World War II, in the same military theater as Norman Mailer. Mattie worked as a prostitute around military bases. The couple divorced in 1948.

At the age of four, Jack entered the first of a series of foster homes ("child labor farms," he called them) as a ward of the state. His father abandoned Mattie and the two children after the war and returned to Texas. By age eleven, Jack, temporarily back with his mother, roamed the streets of Salt Lake, usually with a cigarette hanging from his mouth—already tough and streetwise. For a time, he and Frances were assigned to the foster home of Albert Barlow, a Mormon with five wives and fifty-four children. Jack was then around five or six, and the Barlow tribe became the only "family" he ever truly knew. Even though the boy was considered a Mormon "outsider," he was treated as one of the family and, long afterward, fondly remembered the names of his many "brothers and sisters." While in that Mormon home, his mother visited him regularly. He was baptized into the Mormon faith when he was eight and had reached the "age of accountability." The family patriarch had already served a year's time for bigamy in 1944, and in 1955 Barlow was sent back to prison for the same crime. As Jack put it, "Uncle Albert was sent to prison a second time for practicing his religion." Plural marriage, he wrote, "was the main source of social cohesion in Utah."[3]

After repeatedly running away from all other foster homes, Jack, at the age of eleven or twelve, was sent to the Utah State Industrial School for Boys in Ogden for attempted car theft. Since the age of nine, he had been in and out of juvenile detention for vandalism. Except for one "parole" of sixty days, he remained at the industrial school until the age of eighteen, in 1962. His sister, Frances, gave birth to her first child when she was fifteen. The father was Ben Amador, a tough from their neighborhood who was a promising boxer. Like Jack, Amador was in and out of juvenile detention. He and Frances got married at the Salt Lake County Jail in 1956. Ben went to prison the same day, and Frances gave birth to Ben Amador, Jr., the first of their four children. "He was 18 or 19 when he went to prison," Jack wrote Mailer, "and the year he went to prison he was going to be in the national boxing finals to decide if he would box in the Olympic Games." Ben, a "bad muthafucker" and an Al Pacino look-alike, was the "Duke" of the Utah State Industrial School "long before" Jack arrived. Fighting was a way of life in Utah for working-class Mormon kids. There wasn't a bar "in the two counties of Salt Lake and David" that hadn't heard of Ben. Jack looked up to Ben, but at the same time he resented the Mexican American's carnal knowledge of his sister, for whom the bigoted Jack himself had "incestuous" urges.[4]

Actually, Amador's background was Spanish. Once Jack learned of his Hispanic origins, he accepted Amador, but only as a friend, never as a brother-in-law. He cringed at the thought of any man putting his hands on his sister. Once when Frances visited Jack in prison, bringing Ben along, her husband had to be careful not to touch her in Jack's presence. Afterward, Jack told her never again to bring Ben to visitation. But Ben's presence during visits turned out not to be a problem: in 1980, as Jack's release approached, Frances, his only relative and friend on the "outside," hadn't visited him for the last nine years given the great distances between her home and the federal prisons Jack had been assigned to. For the previous eighteen years, ever since entering adult prison, Jack had written her long letters every two weeks. They became exercises in learning how to write, first by reading his way through the philosophers of the Western world and then by writing in the style of what he read.

"When I started," he told an astonished Mailer in 1979, "I knew about 100 words." He put everything he had into those letters to his sister, details about his treatment in prison, his opinions "on every philosopher from Thales to Wittgenstein . . . For years, and years and again years, I wrote her the way I write you. I don't think anyone has recorded 18 years of his life so thoroughly as I did in those letters." Shortly before writing Mailer in 1979, he had asked his sister just how many letters he had written to her over the nearly twenty-year period, only to learn that the letters, one by one, had gone out with "the daily trash."[5] He was left to wonder whether she had actually even read the letters through, for in her own letters to him she never appeared to address any of their issues. "She has no idea what she has done to me," he told Mailer. To drive home the point, he asked how Mailer would have reacted if his first wife, Beatrice Silverman, had discarded the letters Mailer wrote to her during World War II, which became the basis for *The Naked and the Dead.*

Abbott sometimes got mad at Frances, but he always qualified and ultimately overcame his anger toward her. This daughter of a prostitute was a modest woman who never wore slacks, he said, and who seldom talked about herself in her letters, instead discussing her children and the weather. No one, he told Mailer, could be more discreet. After his capture following his escape in 1971, she traveled all the way from Salt Lake to Denver, over five hundred miles, to visit him. Even though the prison rules allowed an hour's visit for out-of-state visitors, hers that day was limited to ten minutes, after which she left quietly without complaint. After Mailer finally visited Marion in 1979, he told Abbott that the experience (of not being allowed to give Jack a copy of *The Executioner's Song* because the gift hadn't been preapproved) taught him "a little more about prison regulations in a big hurry. I kind of wish it had happened to me while I was writing [*The Executioner's Song*]. It would have given me more understanding of Gilmore's vast rage at the regulations."[6]

Abbott had been reading Mailer's books all his life, he told him. He felt that Mailer had spoken to his generation the way Hemingway and Fitzgerald had spoken to an earlier one. His favorite, at least before *The Executioner's Song*, was *Cannibals and Christians* (1966), a collection of essays on American culture. Jack especially appreciated the surrealistic piece "The Killer: A Story," about a convict's getting out of prison. He also admired *The Fight*, featuring the match between Muhammad Ali and George Foreman in Zaire. "What you've been doing is helping me," Mailer told Abbott on May 10, 1978, while the writer was still at work on *The Executioner's Song*. Mailer had recently been out to Utah to visit Sam Smith, the Draper warden when Gilmore was executed. Smith had refused an interview, and Mailer, he told Abbott, had been thinking "all the while of what you said about Sam . . ."[7] Abbott was bringing Mailer closer and closer to the inmate's point of view of the "pig."

Mailer was deep into his "true life" novel. He had drafted almost 1,200 pages of manuscript by the summer of 1978, basing the novel on the material Larry Schiller had acquired when he secured rights to the condemned man's story. Gilmore, he told Abbott, had written more than 1,500 pages of letters to his girlfriend, Nicole Baker Barrett, in the last few months of his life. At the time, Abbott was being carted around the federal prison system, suspected of taking part in the attempted murder of a prison guard in Atlanta, a charge subsequently dismissed. "I'm locked up in the hole here at the fed joint in Texas, en route back to Lompoc, California," he told Mailer on August 29. It would take another month to get back, since, as he noted, "the prison busses are slow." In his letters he expressed admiration for David Berkowitz, the "Son of Sam" killer, who had terrorized New York City in the bicentennial summer of 1976, randomly shooting point-blank at people sitting in parked cars. Saying he himself would never "pull the trigger" on an innocent person, he blamed society for Berkowitz's crimes.

Abbott also sent Mailer his attempts at writing a play as well as some short stories, all now lost. Writing was frustrating, he said, because it wasn't easy "when you've been raised in a box with 1,000 philosophy books to tell you what life and the world—reality—is all about." Along with absorbing Mailer's literary advice, he occasionally asked Mailer for money so that he could purchase "anything but jail shit." It becomes clear that Abbott had indeed selected Mailer as an escape mechanism after falling out with Kosinski. He hoped to be paroled from the federal system by 1980 or 1981 and then soon after released from his Utah State Prison sentence, the condition placed on the state release stipulating that he leave Utah within twenty-four hours. If he didn't get out soon enough, he feared once he finally got out he might "do something like Gilmore did."[8] Such a comment probably should have given Mailer pause in his effort to help Jack gain freedom, but he doubtless thought, given Abbott's complex prison record, that it would be years before he was likely to be released.

The author and the prisoner wouldn't meet face-to-face until after *The Executioner's Song* was published in 1979. Abbott rather dreaded that meeting, saying that he wasn't "pleasant to look at" and was rather shy. The letters "J-A-C-K" were tattooed on the fingers of his left hand. There was the image of a heart on his left shoulder, as well as a dagger on his forearm. "I talk better on paper," he offered. "I know two languages: prisonese, which is my speaking (vocal) language and English, which is my writing language." Abbott may have helped Mailer reproduce Gary Gilmore's "prisonese," or "gibberish talk," in *The Executioner's Song.* Following the double murders, Gary and another prisoner, Gibbs, while being held in the filthy county jail in Provo, converse in the lingo: "Use a word like figger to say nigger . . . If they said lady from Bristol, that meant pistol . . . Gilmore was talking of ones and twos, and those were shoes. 'Yeah,' said Gilmore to Gibbs, 'A nice pair to go with my fleas and ants.' "[9]

Mailer was working on a ready-made bestseller, Abbott suggested. "It has always been chic to [dig] on mass murderers, crooks, killers of all stripe. America cultivates violence in everything it fashions." "Your book should speak to America," he told his mentor. "Should tell America that if the story of Gary Gilmore entertains them, if they thrill to the violence done *to* as well as *by* Gilmore, then to always be prepared, always have a gun or a cop within reach because it will happen again and again as long as the American traditional system of violence stands above the use of reason in our national life." He went on to compare American shock at the U.S. crime rate to a "worn-out prostitute expressing moral indignation at the thought of pre-marital sexual relations." Abbott was particularly mad at what he called the "American schoolboy intellectuals"—Christians, pacifists, humanists, liberals "who spend their time sniveling about inhumanity at what they see as they shuffle back and forth between the church and the police."[10]

Mailer was writing to Abbott from an office a floor below his Brooklyn apartment at 142 Columbia Heights. Just as he had with *The Naked and the Dead*, he worked in a small space, fully isolated from family and friends. In the case of *The Executioner's Song*, the room resembled a prison cell, with its single window overlooking Brooklyn Heights and the East River. Its view revealed giant cranes unloading and loading ocean freighters. As his biographer J. Michael Lennon writes, he came in this tight space to know Gilmore as well as he knew his ex-wives. Now in full correspondence with Jack Abbott, he was ready to pick up the pace of his masterpiece. There would be as many characters, indeed four or five times as many, in it as there had been in his first book and bestseller, *The Naked and the Dead*.[11]

Abbott's letters immersed Mailer in the mood of the incarcerated; they pulled him into a personality that had been formed in prison—that had painfully and agonizingly matured through puberty and adolescence into manhood, all in a cage. Gary Gilmore's story simply wasn't enough to have plunged this talented writer into his greatest literary achievement. Schiller's death row interview of Gilmore in *Playboy* gives us a glimpse into the relatively superficial character of Mailer's subject, who died by Utah firing squad at the age of thirty-six (Abbott's age at the time of his initial correspondence with Mailer). Gilmore had spent only three of his last twenty-two years on the outside.

> *PLAYBOY:* When was the last time you were out of jail at Christmas?
>
> GILMORE: Nineteen sixty-one.
>
> *PLAYBOY:* A long time ago.
>
> GILMORE: Yeah. It's like what W. C. Fields said: "All things being equal, I'd rather not spend Christmas in prison." [Laughs]

The fateful release, during which Gilmore killed two men in cold blood, had lasted only three months. Although Gilmore shared with Abbott a particular talent—in Gilmore's case, graphic artistry—he lacked the intellectual background Abbott had acquired in prison. Also a stutterer, Gilmore frequently complained about the constant prison noise: "It's so goddamn *noisy* in here today, I can't think," he said during the *Playboy* interview, to which Schiller retorted, "Perhaps the noise is part of your sentence."

Gilmore found relief in his new fame as a willing victim of capital punishment. Because of the publicity he garnered by insisting on being executed, he received up to a thousand letters a day—and a total of more than forty thousand, which were sent to the Utah State Prison. Answering about fifty letters a day and even autographing Bibles sent to him, he occasionally joked about his impending death. Playing off a Timex television commercial popular in the 1970s, in which famed newscaster (now forgotten) John Cameron Swayze dips the watch in water to discover it still ticking, Gilmore told *Playboy*: "After I fall over, [Swayze] can be wearin' a stethoscope; he can put it on my heart and say, 'Well, that stopped.' And then he can put the stethoscope on the Timex [Laughs] and say, 'She's still runnin', folks.' "[12]

6

The Prison Movement in the 1970s

"There's an attitude now in America," Norman Mailer said during his disastrous press conference on January 21, 1982, following the conviction of Jack Abbott for first-degree manslaughter. "Let's bring the law and order, let's get rid of all these criminals, all these people who knife people, who shoot people—it's too easy."[1] He was reflecting on the end of an era of prison reform in which a multitude of educational programs were available to hard-core prisoners in America—an ending brought about in large part by the fact that Abbott, a beneficiary of such programs, had killed after being released from prison. The educational opportunities in prison had found their genesis in the 1960s, when the civil rights movement encouraged more than a few black prisoners to see themselves not as criminals but as "slaves" in racist America. Prison reforms had also come about because of the Vietnam protest movement, in which so many blacks were drafted into the military and killed in a war against what President Lyndon Johnson had once dismissed as a "piss-ant country."

The voices of protest in the 1960s led to what came to be known as "radical chic," a term coined by the writer Tom Wolfe in a special issue of *New York* magazine of June 9, 1970, to mock the rich's newfound interest in the underdog. Its catalyst was the Park Avenue penthouse party for the Black Panthers hosted by Felicia and Leonard Bernstein, a party in line with similar efforts by the American elite to support radical causes: Jane Fonda's visit to Hanoi and American prisoners of war, the Yale chaplain William Sloane Coffin's outspokenness on Vietnam. In general, the political fantasies of the rich eventually moved from civil rights to the Vietnam War and, as the war wound down, to prison reform.

Ironically, the prison movement got its start at almost the same time such hopes of improvement in our prisons began to diminish. Two days after the widely publicized Bernstein party, Senator Daniel Patrick Moynihan quietly told President Richard Nixon that the issue of race in America would benefit from a large dose of "benign neglect."[2] The movement began properly with the publication of George Jackson's prison letters in 1970 and the author's violent death in prison a year later. Like Jack Abbott, George Jackson entered adult prison at eighteen and was personally and politically redeemed through the works of Marx, Lenin, Trotsky, Engels, and Mao. Sent to Soledad State Prison in California for robbing a gas station of seventy dollars, he foolishly agreed to plead guilty for the promise of a brief stint in the county jail. "But," as he wrote in *Soledad Brother: The Prison Letters of George Jackson*, "when time came for sentencing they tossed me into the penitentiary with one to life." That was in 1960, and every year after that when he came up for parole, he was turned down, until it looked as though he would serve a life sentence.

The publication of his prison letters caused an international sensation almost overnight. They chronicled the painful evaporation of Jackson's hope for freedom and his discovery of Marxism, which allowed him to think of himself and his fellow, mainly black, prisoners as victims of American neoslavery less than a hundred years after the Emancipation Proclamation. "If there is a God, Mama, he hate me," Jackson wrote in the early stages of his prison education, when his parole was repeatedly put off. With the same intensity and clarity as Abbott, Jackson eloquently analyzed prison conditions as he condemned them, claiming that "the great majority of Soledad pigs are southern migrants who do not want to work in the fields and farms of the area, who couldn't sell cars or insurance . . ." In short, they were the lackeys of the whites, the former Europeans who tried to colonize the world and were now colonizing a massive black penal colony in America. "The events of the Congo, Vietnam, Malaya, Korea and here in the U.S.," he told his father, "are taking place all for the same reasons. The commotion, the violence, the struggles in all these areas and many more spring from one source, the evil and malign, possessive and greedy Europeans."[3]

Historical connections were made between American slavery and the beginnings of the penitentiary system—what Eldridge Cleaver, who, while still in prison, corresponded with Mailer, would call in *Soul on Ice* "a continuation of slavery on a higher plane."[4] If not victims of the sharecropper system in the South, American blacks were arrested for vagrancy and essentially re-enslaved on chain gangs. Marxist theory saw prisons as primarily economic commodities. The role of literature in unmasking prison's ulterior motives, therefore, was paramount. Not only did the argument condemn prison conditions—indeed, prisons themselves—but it celebrated the articulate nature of prison writers, longtime prisoners who had otherwise been discarded by society. As Angela Davis, who corresponded with Jackson in prison, noted in *Are Prisons Obsolete?,* "numerous works authored by prisoners followed the 1970 publication of George Jackson's *Soledad Brother.* While many prison writers . . . had discovered the emancipatory potential of writing on their own, relying either on the education they had received prior to their imprisonment or on their tenacious efforts at self-education, others pursued their writing as a direct result of prison educational programs during the era [of the 1970s]."[5]

During the first half of the 1970s, college-level programs spread to 350 prisons in forty-five states. These were funded in large part by Pell Grants (abolished for prisoners in the 1990s but restored in 2016 by the Obama administration), the National Endowment for the Arts, PEN American Center's Prison Writing Program, the Black Cultural Coalition's Prison Arts Program, and smaller entities sponsoring workshops, performances, and literary competitions. Departments of correction around the country engaged in other prisoner programs with their state arts commissions.[6] By the 1980s, most of these programs had disappeared. Punishment replaced rehabilitation as the goal of most state and federal systems. After Abbott, prison writers were largely seen as merely gifted con artists. The liberal press and literary organizations were urged to give up their efforts at prison reform. Art, it was declared, was not the way to redeem criminal minds. Instead, art education programs ought to be directed to law-abiding citizens who could not afford college. Thus, state and federal funds for prison education and rehabilitation dried up. State funds for public universities also began to dry up, as tuition rates rose four- or fivefold by the turn of the twenty-first century.

George Jackson, who, as he wrote, first read Marx in prison, was the founder of the Black Guerilla Family, which still exists in and out of prisons today. Although the movement allegedly sought to include white prisoners, it consisted mostly, if not exclusively, of those who were black and brown. This division was reinforced by the "progressive lawyers," public defenders who saw minority prisoners as "political prisoners" and dismissed white inmates as simply criminals. Abbott was painfully aware that he wasn't a true part of prison protest, which, because of the civil rights movement, if not the Vietnam protest movement, was minority-based. "Nobody can ever call me comrade," he told Mailer while referring to the "BGF" on October 8, 1978, "and at the same time condone in any way hatred of white people and vice versa." When Jackson spoke of prison as a "neo-slave" existence, he wasn't referring to white prisoners. Jackson may even have viewed himself as an "enslaved" Martin Luther King, whom he admired even while disagreeing with King's concept of nonviolence. Otherwise, Jackson sounds in his letters much like Henry David Thoreau in his "Essay on Civil Disobedience," whose mind, in spite of his incarcerated body, walked free.

Once his prison letters were published, Jackson probably became a marked man by prison officials. They were no doubt doubly concerned about the Jackson influence when, in August 1970, Jackson's younger brother Jonathan, who had just turned seventeen, single-handedly entered the Marin County Courthouse, armed with a satchel full of handguns, a shotgun, and an assault rifle. "All right, gentleman," the teenager announced, "hold it right there. I'm taking over now." James McClain, a black prisoner, was in court for assaulting a guard. Young Jackson gave a pistol to McClain, who then taped the sawed-off shotgun to the neck of the presiding judge. Then Jackson and McClain also took as hostages the district attorney and three jurors. During their exit from the building, the black assembly, soon to be known as the "Soledad Brothers," was cut down in a hail of bullets from the Marin County police and forces from nearby San Quentin, where George Jackson was currently incarcerated. Jonathan Jackson and McClain, along with the judge and two other prisoners who had joined the escape, were killed. The DA was wounded and paralyzed for life. Miraculously, none of the three female jurors were seriously injured. As some of the weapons used in the assault had been purchased by Angela Davis, an activist and at the time a UCLA professor, she was charged with "aggravated kidnapping and first degree murder in the death of Judge Harold Haley." Her fleeing and capture and subsequent acquittal further called attention to prison unrest, especially after the five-day riot at Attica State Facility in September of 1971, in which twenty-nine prisoners and ten guards were killed.[7]

George Jackson was killed at San Quentin weeks before Attica during an alleged escape attempt; he was twenty-nine. As the author of letters as provocative as Abbott's *In the Belly of the Beast*, Jackson became a martyr to the literary prison movement. In fact, Abbott's own successful escape from prison the same year was inspired by Jackson. It was, he wrote, Jackson's "living example that fired me and other 'rebels' in prisons all across the country."[8] Here, Abbott was also sounding the broader complaint about prison, seeing its source in the advancement of a capitalist system and thus bringing him closer to the issues addressed by African American incarcerated writers. So far, the only other famous prison "white" writer was Caryl Chessman, a convicted rapist who was executed in 1960 and whose *Cell 2455 Death Row* had helped propel the banning of executions in the United States in 1963. Abbott, whose mixed-race background never changed his profile as a white prisoner, didn't go to prison for a violent crime, but, as he would argue in his 1981 trial, he had gone there as a "state-raised" convict. He was in prison, he argued, because of his unfortunate beginnings with a prostitute for a mother and a drunk for a father who abandoned him. He had been "born" into prison—first into foster homes, then reform schools, and finally adult prison. His only violent crime had been *in* prison *in self-defense*. So even though he felt cut off from the black prison protest, he was potentially one of their strongest voices. Like Etheridge Knight, Jimmy Santiago Baca, and Miguel Piñero, three minority prisoners whose works won wide acclaim, Jack Abbott learned to write in prison.

Along with Leonard Bernstein, Norman Mailer was regarded as one of the agents of "radical chic" after the Abbott debacle. His mentorship of Abbott can be compared to Bob Dylan's support of Rubin "Hurricane" Carter, William F. Buckley's efforts to get Edgar Smith out of jail, Jean Paul Sartre's support of Jean Genet, and William Styron's mentorship of James Blake. For Mailer, it wasn't so much about white guilt as a fear of fascism—a theme that originates in *The Naked and the Dead* and is argued through stick characters in *Barbary Shore*. By the 1970s, with his involvement in the Gilmore and Abbott cases, he saw its threat most notably in American prisons and the "throw away the key" mentality of the Nixon years. Moreover, Mailer's admiration of Hemingway's macho characters and marginalized types in his essay "The White Negro" (1959), suggests, as Michiko Kakutani writes, Mailer's identity with people on the margins who assert themselves in the face of unfairness and "kill without apology"—characteristics equated not only with virility but also creativity.[9]

Gary Gilmore brought back executions in America, and Jack Henry Abbott helped bring back the public wrath against prisoners. Rehabilitation programs were now deemed either too expensive or ineffective.

7

His Own Voice

As noted earlier, Abbott was able to initiate a correspondence with Jerzy Kosinski because the author of *The Painted Bird* was president of PEN during its prison program in the 1970s. Ordinarily, it would have been difficult to impossible to get the attention of a famous author, especially someone as prominent as Kosinski or Mailer, also a president of PEN after Kosinski. Both writers were regularly asked to read or endorse somebody's book. Abbott's hook in Norman's case was to mention in his first letter that he had been personally acquainted with Gary Gilmore. Possibly, Abbott and Gilmore knew each other vaguely at Marion, where each had served time for bank robbery. Moreover, Abbott had served time in the same Utah state prison at "Point of the Mountain," where Gilmore was executed in 1977. Abbott, as he told Mailer in his first letter, deemed Gilmore "a good convict" like himself—somebody who was no "punk." He insisted on the difference between a "convict" and an "inmate"—one who sought the protection of another convict by becoming his "wife." Each man came to the federal penitentiary at Marion from state prisons—Gilmore from Oregon State Prison and Abbott from the

Utah one in Draper. Both men had Mormon roots and connections. In *The Executioner's Song,* Gilmore, however, is not the "good convict" Abbott paints but, according to Mailer, did "not rank high on any self-respecting convict's scale. He would be looked upon not as a heavy, but a ding. Sufficiently unpredictable for other convicts to give him a wide berth, but not a convict with real clout on the inside."[1]

Abbott's information must have been of immediate interest to Mailer as he struggled to put together and make sense of the massive amount of material for Gilmore's story—testimonials, tape recordings, interviews, criminal records, a *Playboy* interview (the longest in the magazine's history until that time). Mailer's debt to Abbott was "sizeable." He told the press after Abbott's manslaughter conviction that the prisoner "helped me a great deal with *The Executioner's Song.*" In the afterword to the novel, he described Abbott as "a convict who has spent much of his life in Western prisons [and sent him] a series of letters . . . that delineate the code, morals, the anguish, the philosophy, the pitfalls, the pride, and the search for inviolability of hard-line convicts in language whose equal I have not encountered in prison literature." He thought Abbott's book as potentially powerful as Eldridge Cleaver's *Soul on Ice.* Mailer visited Oregon State Prison more than once during the composition of his book, to interview guards and prisoners who had known Gilmore before he became famous for demanding his own execution, becoming his own special version of a "dead man walking." But no one gave him more insight into this man than Abbott, who had lived nearly the same life. Even those most closely involved with Gilmore during his three fateful months of freedom leading up to the Utah murders—his girlfriend, Nicole Baker Barrett; his favorite cousin and parole sponsor, Brenda Nicol; Brenda's father, Vern Damico, who gave his nephew a job upon his release; and Gilmore's mother—could not provide glimpses into the mind of the convict more insightful than could a convict with true writing talent. In doing so, Abbott, through his letters to Mailer, became the author of one of the most powerful prison narratives in American literature, a modern-day tour of Dante's inferno called *In the Belly of the Beast*.[2]

As Abbott began his correspondence with Mailer in 1978, he compared himself to Gilmore. They were both "old school," he wrote, in the sense that when they entered prison a slim majority of the inmates were white. Pigs were pigs, and snitching on one another was the deadliest of sins. He blamed the change on the civil rights movement, after which a man was judged, he said, by his race instead of his principles. Previously, the penitentiaries were tough because the guards made it tough. If you engaged in any kind of conversation with one, it could endanger your life. He said that what had become the case for (white) men like Gilmore and Abbott was that the toughest prisons were now reserved for those who were not "socially disadvantaged" by race, while the minorities received relatively shorter sentences. George Jackson would have disagreed.

Both Gilmore and Abbott were deeply resentful of what they considered the favored treatment of racial minorities by prison authorities. In *The Executioner's Song*, where the ACLU and the

NAACP file suit to prevent Gilmore's execution, the condemned man rails against both organizations. "You [the NAACP] and ACLU are flip-flops. You take one stand on abortion, which is actually execution. . . . And then you take another stand on capital punishment." The NAACP felt that the resumption of execution with Gilmore would unleash a torrent of black executions, which it did. "NAACP, look boy," Gilmore told an imagined representative of the organization, quoted in *The Salt Lake Tribune*, "I am a white man. Get that through your Brillo Pad heads, boy. I know a lot of black dudes, and I don't know any who respect the dumb niggers of the NAACP. . . . Butt out, you punks."[3]

Abbott thought there remained only a few strongholds of such "old school" convicts who actually both respected and feared one another. United States Penitentiary, Leavenworth, he said, was one of them, and Marion was surely another. But, even there, "fresh blood" was beginning to flood the place, so that in a few more years such idealized cons were about to become a thing of the past. Abbott's nostalgia for a time that probably never existed suggests how remotely connected he was to the actual day-to-day world outside prison and how he—and Gilmore—were unprepared for freedom, which in both cases lasted almost exactly only three months. Interestingly, in *The Executioner's Song* Mailer stayed almost completely away from the subject of race—except for Gilmore's fiction of having killed a black bully in prison. In the conversations of the working class in Orem and Provo, where Gilmore's two murders happened, there is no trace of racism. But that may have been accurate in the sense that Utah is, even today, nearly 92 percent white. The blacks that Abbott encountered were in the federal prisons, where he had spent the last seven years before his release in 1981.

Abbott continued his correspondence from the federal prison in Lompoc, California. There, he told Mailer that he had just gotten loaded on "some good weed" and had his picture taken, which he promised to send. It was the first prison, he said, in which inmates had been able or allowed to have their images taken. "Hell, in Leavenworth," he added, "it is illegal to even have any pictures of yourself, even pictures taken before you came to prison!" Prisoners were stripped of more than simply their freedom. Told what to wear, what to eat, how long to eat ("sit—grab—gobble—stand—file out"); caged the majority of their waking hours; and often submerged in the suffocation of solitary, prisoners were reduced, it was intended, to automatons.[4] In spite of every effort he ever made to avoid becoming embittered, Abbott confessed that he had failed. As a result, Abbott was the turbocharge to Mailer's characterization of Gary Gilmore, who had also been in prison since adolescence, and as Abbott wrote of himself, been incarcerated so long that "your fantasies of the free world are no longer easily distinguished from what you 'know' the free world is really like. So long that being free is exactly identical to a freeman's dreams of heaven. To die and go to the free world." That was what Gilmore chose, when he traded more prison time (on death row, in this case, during a period when executions were indefinitely on hold) for a shot in the heart.

Life in prison was one long nightmare in which the mind alone wandered in the "free world." It was the part of the prisoner that never truly saw or felt "*actual* objects but which lives and roves through . . . passions and emotions." Prison was taking Abbott further and further away from his life on earth. Talking to Mailer about prison life released Abbott's literary "voice." "I don't ever talk of these feelings," he told Mailer on October 8, 1978, in a neat and steady hand in a letter that went on for pages and pages, recto and verso of unlined, now slightly yellowed sheets. "In fact, I'm only now thinking of it (as I write this). I find it very painful to look in the mirror. When I walk past a glass window in a corridor and happen to see my reflection, I get angry on impulse. I feel shame and hatred at such times." When forced "by circumstance" into a crowd of other prisoners, it was all he could do to keep from attacking somebody. Bottled up within him were hostility and hatred without a specific target, and Mailer must—or *should*—have wondered whether this encaged genius could ever be safely freed. Would he turn into Gary Gilmore, who within three months of his release from prison, had killed?

Abbott claimed that he never actively sought confrontation in prison encounters. In fact, he had, he said, to "intentionally gauge his voice in conversation" to hide his pent-up anger. He blamed it all on prison. It had shaped him since reform school. It was a form of paranoia, born of a lifetime of petty restrictions and seemingly arbitrary punishments. "Imagine a thousand daily intrusions on your life every hour and minute of every day and you can grasp the source of this paranoia, this anger that could consume me at any moment if I ever lost control." *The Executioner's Song* opens and closes with what Mailer calls "an old prison rhyme"—in actuality a poem he wrote years earlier—that reflects Abbott's bitterness:

Deep in my dungeon
I welcome you here
Deep in my dungeon
I worship your fear
Deep in my dungeon
I dwell
I do not know
If I wish you well.

In *The Executioner's Song*, after twelve or more years in adult prison, following his teen years in reform school (after burglarizing, by his own admission, at least sixty residences), Gilmore is released to his cousin Brenda and his uncle Vern. As he removes his plastic prison shoes to prepare to spend his first night of freedom on Brenda's foldout couch, Mailer describes Gilmore in his "true-life novel" as standing beside her with an "impish little grin" and asking his cousin, "Do you know how long it's been since I slept on a sheet?"[5]

Abbott concluded his letter to Mailer that day by saying that nobody had the right to "take Jack Abbott away from Jack Abbott," saying in effect what he would bitterly tell Ed Bradley during his 1982 interview on *60 Minutes*. Yet that was what was being done to him: "I've become a stranger to my needs and desires. I've seen those around me through the years fall apart morally, seen them go mad in subtle ways and seen them surrender their will to the routine of prison and I have resisted it all much, much longer than others." All the while, Mailer was listening intently as he consumed letter after letter from Federal Prisoner 87098-132. The author, overwhelmed with daily details of ex-wives, children, the IRS, and demands from Little, Brown that he get back to *Ancient Evenings* (1983), the book for which he had already been given annual chunks of the original advance, seldom responded, having his secretary Judith McNally tell Abbott that all her boss's writing these days was going into *The Executioner's Song.* She assured Abbott he was reading his letters, and she told Abbott that they were helping Mailer write his book. Perhaps not altogether truthfully, Jack said that it was the sole reason he had written Mailer in the first place—simply to help him get the real prison on record in his Gilmore book. "I'm just giving you the cosmogony of life where myself and Gilmore exist so that it can help you understand. There are a million small things, details of psychological and physical things in the world I hope I've cast light on for you."

He cautioned Mailer not to write a book like Truman Capote's *In Cold Blood* (1966). Abbott wasn't specific about his objections to Capote's novel, but he did say that the danger in writing about prison and convicts was that, at some point, out of fear or repulsion, intellectuals break off from the subject, failing to see in their subject matter something worthy of sympathy if not compassion. "It eludes them that at the heart of justice is vengeance." In writing *The Executioner's Song*, he said, Mailer ought to bear in mind that the main crime of Gilmore and himself was "knowing hard times."[6] He hadn't read much about Gilmore, but he didn't have to. He knew his doppelganger's dilemma from the inside out—trapped from childhood in a pattern of parental neglect, misbehavior, and crime. He had read, however, the 1977 *Playboy* interview with Larry Schiller. There, Gilmore had described himself and others like him as eternal recidivists—"We're creatures of habit, man." His longest stretch of freedom between reform school and imprisonment as a habitual criminal in 1964 amounted to eight months. At age thirty-six he had spent nearly nineteen of his last twenty-two years behind bars. Like Abbott, those years had one break, during a brief escape in 1972. Gilmore's life otherwise had been regulated by impulse. He couldn't say why he had killed, only that if freed he might do it again.[7] Gilmore lacked what prison psychologists called "impulse control."

8

State-Raised Convict

After saying all along to Mailer that he had no ulterior motives in helping him with the Gilmore saga, Abbott complained in a letter of October 22, 1978, that his case in prison was "hopeless," mainly because, aside from his sister, he had no outside help. One wonders whether Frances truly wanted Jack out again, perhaps knowing his feelings for her and those against her husband. "She is all I have," he wrote, "and she is really not worth it." Abbott, as he indicated, was seemingly stuck in prison for life for cashing a check on a depleted bank account (which ignores, of course, the fact that the checks themselves had been stolen and that he had stabbed another prisoner to death, escaped prison, and robbed a bank). He hoped that Mailer wouldn't fall off his desk if he asked for "40 or 50 dollars a month for a while," a request to which Mailer quietly complied. The two writers were also approaching the useful end of Jack's letters, because Mailer had a deadline to deliver *The Executioner's Song* to Little, Brown in six weeks, by December of that year.

In his ploy, Jack offered, in a letter of November 1, 1978, to conclude their correspondence without any financial compensation, saying he had exhausted its original purpose. Yet to hint at his longstanding need of a savior, he went on to talk about a black woman named Tangerine to whom he had similarly poured out his prison woes years before. She was apparently an aspiring television comedian for whom Abbott claimed he had provided jokes during their correspondence. When he finally got around to asking her for the kind of help he was now asking Mailer for, he said she took instant offense. Having no funds for the basics of soap or toothpaste, let alone "a cup of coffee or real cigarettes," he had dared to ask her for help since she had ended one of her twice-weekly letters saying to be sure to let her know if he "needed anything." "She wrote me a haughty letter (I am in a strip cell so fucked up even the visual sight of a piece of colored cloth—red, bright colors moved me to euphoria) telling me I 'surprised' her and that she did not like 'materialists.'" He wrote back in a "frenzy," beseeching her not to abandon him, but he got back only more scented letters in which she talked about her own problems. When you are so down that you will cling to anyone out there, "you hit bottom." Yet in prison on an endless sentence, there really was no bottom; you fall through it "forever if you do not grab one of them, no matter how slimy."

Two days earlier, however, he had gone before the parole board, which for unknown reasons (perhaps to get rid of a troublemaker) moved up his release date from Marion from 1990 to June 1980—then eighteen months in the future. That meant that he would be "paroled" from federal prison but would have to serve out the remainder of his Utah State Prison sentence unless it too was shortened. "When I get to Utah in 1980," he told Mailer on November 9, 1978, "I will have served 18 solid years. Two more years will give me 20 years and I feel they will set me free if I leave the state within 24 hours and promise never to return." Even though he faced a relatively long stretch before such a release, which was also conditioned on his conduct record between now and then, it made him euphoric. "I will be a free man (legally) in this country before my life is over."

Meanwhile, Judith McNally, Mailer's secretary, apparently lost most of the letters of the first three months of the Abbott-Mailer correspondence in 1978, material that was to be the specific basis for what would become *In the Belly of the Beast*. The chain-smoking McNally tried to apologize and reason with Abbott, but he remained furious, telling Mailer of a four-page rant he had sent her. She was, he said, somewhat ambiguously, "just another example of what it is about women I do not like; what it is that repulses me in them."

Abbott followed up on November 17 with a 2,800-word essay worthy of the title "The Confession of a State-Raised Convict," or "The Hope of a State-Raised Convict." This particular kind of convict, he wrote, is a prisoner who grows up from boyhood to manhood in penal institutions. As a consequence, he moves into adulthood with a case of "arrested adolescence." Often, college students are seen as delayed adolescents living out their last free years outside the "real world." But they are nevertheless moving on to the threshold of the "real world." Indeed, their contacts in school are dry runs for the competitive markets they will enter as college graduates, whereas prison contacts usually offer up only a curriculum of crime. After graduation, society gives college graduates the respect as a "man," and their judgments gradually gain respect. They mature both socially and emotionally.

"It is not true for the state-raised convict," Abbott painfully told Mailer. "As a boy in reform school, he is punished for being a little boy. In prison, he is punished for being a man. It is assumed the objects convicts pursue are adolescent. A prisoner who is not state-raised, i.e., serving only one or two short sentences, tolerates the situation just because of his natural social maturity prior to incarceration. He knows things (relations) are different outside prison."

Not so for the others, who have no idea of such a difference. "They have no conception because they have no experience and, hence, no maturity. Their judgment is untempered, rash; their emotions are impulsive, raw, unmellowed." This distinction probably led Mailer in his characterization of Gary Gilmore, whose impulsiveness culminated in murders he could not adequately explain. In two successive days, Gilmore shot two innocent men in the head as they lay on the ground with their hands behind their backs because he didn't want to kill his girlfriend, Nicole, who had refused to see him anymore because of their latest quarrel. "This one is for me," he allegedly whispered when he put the first of two bullets into the skull of Max Jensen at the Sinclair gas station in Orem, Utah, on July 19, 1976. The second shot, he recalled saying, "is for Nicole."[1]

Mailer echoed Abbott's essay when he quoted the Mormon prison chaplain who vividly complained that the prison system is a

> complete socialist way of life. No wonder Gilmore had gotten into trouble. For twelve years, a prison had told him when to go to bed and when to eat, what to wear and when to get up. [His prison surroundings were] diametrically opposed to the capitalist environment. Then one day they put the convict out the front door, told him today is magic, at two o'clock you are a capitalist. Now, do it on your own. Go out, find a job, get up by yourself, report to work on time, manage your money, do all the things you were taught not to do in prison. Guaranteed to fail. Eighty percent went back to jail.[2]

Throughout *The Executioner's Song,* we follow Gilmore down the inevitable path of failure. When Brenda and her husband, Johnny, meet him at the Salt Lake airport after his flight from Illinois and the Marion federal penitentiary, Gary is mildly intoxicated, having drunk too many minibottles of liquor given him by the hostesses on his plane. As they drive south to Orem on Interstate 91, they eerily pass "Point of the Mountain." On the other side, in the desert, stands Utah State Prison in Draper, where in less than a year Gary will be shot in the heart. Already something of an alcoholic from drinking prison beer, or "pruno," a watery brew made from bread that at first tastes like vomit, he takes to stealing beer from convenience stores in broad daylight—just walking out with either a six-pack or a case as if he had already paid. The graphic artist in him in prison vanishes as he tries to inhale all his freedom at once. Vern remarks that he acts as though he is twenty instead of thirty-six, not "much older when he said good-bye to the world for thirteen years."[3] It is just a matter of time before the petty crimes of this impulsive "free man" turn to violent ones.

In the "prison regime," Abbott continued, underlining for emphasis, everything was "*either/or.*" You either submitted or were punished. "*You are only allowed to submit. . . . You are a rebellious adolescent who must obey and submit to the judgment of 'grown-ups'—tyrants.*" Just as a teenager is denied the keys to the family car for any disobedience, Abbott wrote, "I am subjected to the hole for *any* disobedience, any mischief." He would "go to the hole for murder as well as [for] stealing a packet of sugar." Speaking of solitary confinement with its starvation diets and the rush of the "goon-squad" using tear gas against all resistance, Abbott posed the question that must have haunted Mailer as he completed and revised *The Executioner's Song*: "What do such atrocities do to the judgment of a child who spends his entire life behind bars? What does it do to the judgment, in other words, of a man who knows nothing else?"

At thirty-four, Abbott confessed to Mailer in a letter dated November 1, 1978, "I am barely a precocious child." Citing Carl Jung and Alfred Adler, he explained away his homosexual activity in prison (and his misogyny) by saying that everybody is bisexual before "maturity," a stage the state-raised convict is not allowed to reach. For such a prisoner, the emotions don't necessarily develop with the body, "the genitals, the glands, etc." They never reach "puberty."

In *The New York Review of Books* of July 11, 1981, he wrote of his five years in reform school, from age twelve to seventeen, that "It really was years, many years, before I began to actually realize that the women in my life . . . were not women, but men; years before I assimilated the notion that this was unnatural." The "soft, pretty girls" who "giggled and teased" him, his "several wives"—all the sexual love he had enjoyed had been revealed to be a sham as far as he was concerned. It struck him like "a hammer blow" to his temple that the world "could so intimately betray" him. It wasn't, he added, that he had been actually fooled to believe his lovers were female. He knew the physical difference, but he also believed that "this was a natural sex that emerged with the society of men"—that the same-sex attraction also existed in "the society of women as well."[4]

To men like himself who had been shut off from the "free world," from its breadth of possibilities, Abbott wrote and Mailer underscored, "the essence of reason in human affairs is force." In other words, the "force of nature" includes violence, which inside prison is the only "force of reason" available. This was the state-raised convict's conception of manhood—violence. To Mailer, it must have seemed like talking to Gary Gilmore himself, as Abbott explained both himself and Gilmore from the inside out. For Gilmore, life meant you took what you needed. When in need of money to purchase a car, for example, Gilmore asks a friend in *The Executioner's Song* to help him rob a bank, seemingly disregarding completely the consequences of its sending him back to the life in prison he hated. Seeing himself ultimately as a victim of injustice, the state-raised convict exonerates himself of any fault in committing violence to survive. Killing Richard Adan, Abbott maintained, was an "accident," the result of twenty years in prison. He had felt threatened and responded automatically—his prison impulse for survival simply overwhelming him.

In his letters to Mailer, Abbott frequently described the minutiae of prison life. On November 29, 1978, he spoke of "all manner of dope [that] flows so freely at Lompoc." A newcomer wouldn't even notice it because everybody handled it so well. "I, for example, have been so smashed I could hardly stand erect but when I sense a pig I can appear normal." The "dope" consisted of angel dust, heroin, "mini-bennies" (done by injection), marijuana, and hashish, which was smoked. He was just "coming around" from an assortment of such drugs when he began his letter to Mailer that day. The gradual sobriety brought him back to the world of prison and its unhappiness. Unhappy, he said, because he still had hope of becoming free. And yet as the prospect of freedom became real, it also became frightening. Formerly, with no hope of release in a near future, he could rack up all the disciplinary offenses he chose; anyway, the quiet of solitary in federal prison was preferable to the noise in the general population for reflection and writing. But with a parole date in sight, he feared screwing up and blowing this latest chance.

Abbott's subject matter in his letters to Mailer spanned mod-

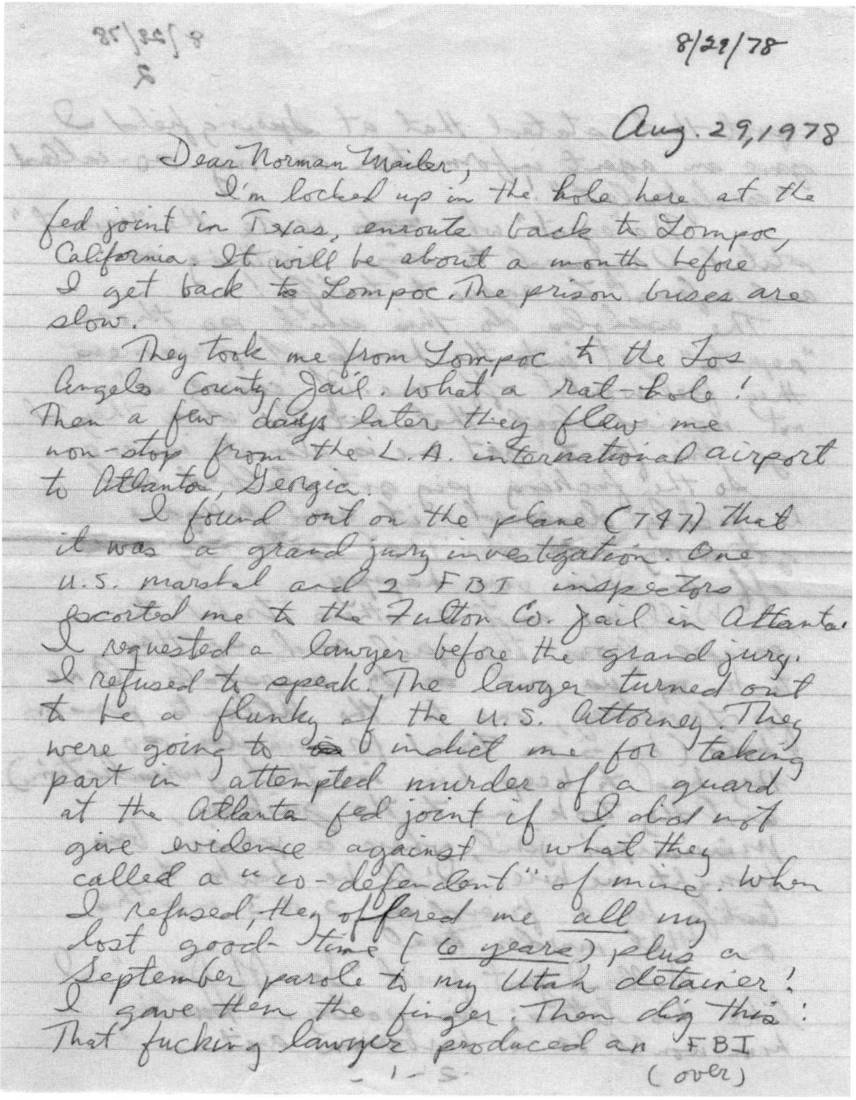

8/29/78

Aug. 29, 1978

Dear Norman Mailer,

I'm locked up in the hole here at the fed joint in Texas, enroute back to Lompoc, California. It will be about a month before I get back to Lompoc. The prison buses are slow.

They took me from Lompoc to the Los Angeles County Jail. What a rat-hole! Then a few days later they flew me non-stop from the L.A. international airport to Atlanta, Georgia.

I found out on the plane (747) that it was a grand jury investigation. One U.S. marshal and 2 FBI inspectors escorted me to the Fulton Co. Jail in Atlanta. I requested a lawyer before the grand jury. I refused to speak. The lawyer turned out to be a flunky of the U.S. Attorney. They were going to indict me for taking part in attempted murder of a guard at the Atlanta fed joint if I did not give evidence against what they called a "co-defendant" of mine. When I refused, they offered me all my lost good-time (6 years) plus a September parole to my Utah detainer! I gave them the finger. Then dig this: That fucking lawyer produced an FBI

- 1 -

(over)

Letter from Jack Henry Abbott (first page) to Norman Mailer, August 29, 1978. *(Harry Ransom Center, The University of Texas at Austin)*

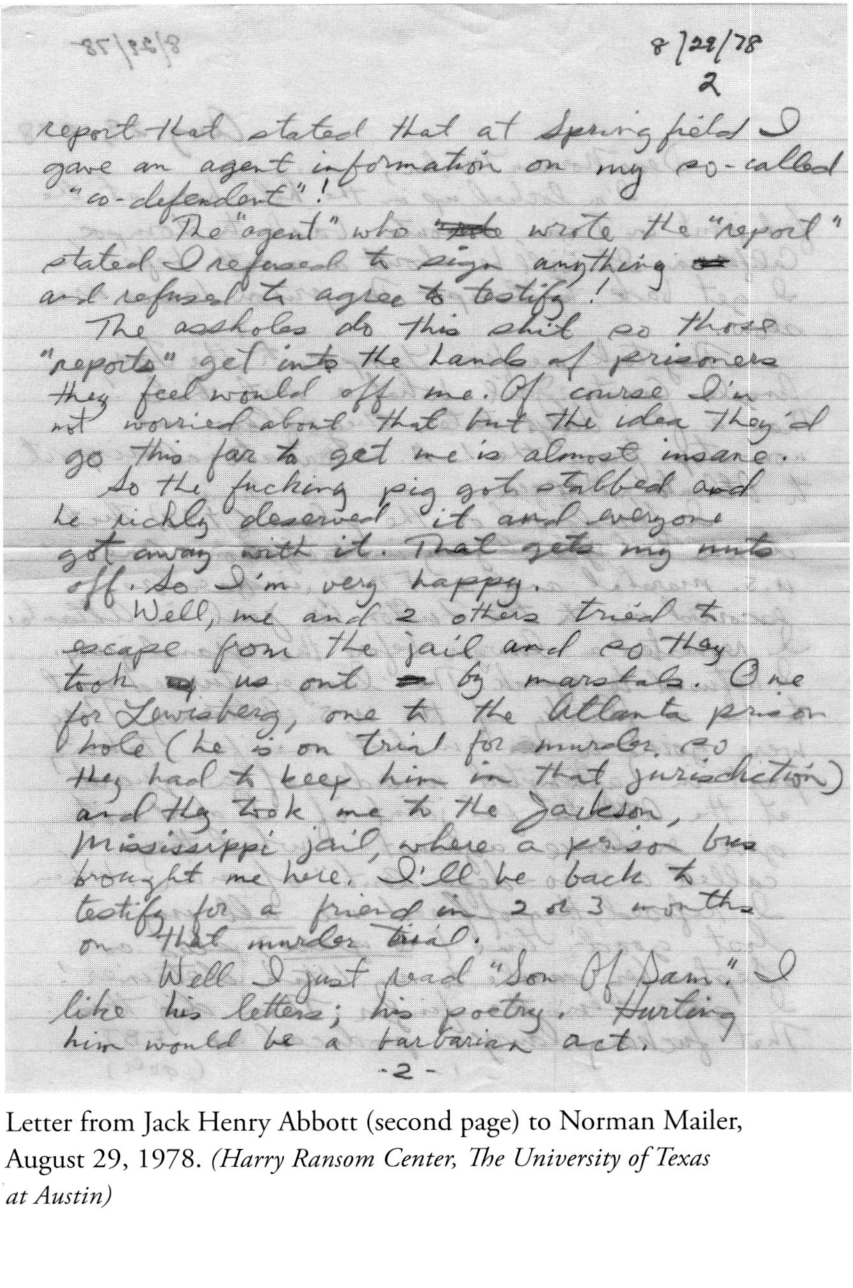
8/29/78
2

report that stated that at Springfield I gave an agent information on my so-called "co-defendant"!

The "agent" who wrote the "report" stated I refused to sign anything and refused to agree to testify!

The assholes do this shit so those "reports" get into the hands of prisoners they feel would off me. Of course I'm not worried about that but the idea they'd go this far to get me is almost insane.

So the fucking pig got stabbed and he richly deserved it and everyone got away with it. That gets my nuts off. So I'm very happy.

Well, me and 2 others tried to escape from the jail and so they took us out by marshals. One for Lewisburg, one to the Atlanta prison hole (he is on trial for murder so they had to keep him in that jurisdiction) and they took me to the Jackson, Mississippi jail, where a prison bus brought me here. I'll be back to testify for a friend in 2 or 3 months on that murder trial.

Well I just read "Son Of Sam". I like his letters; his poetry. Hurting him would be a barbarian act.

-2-

Letter from Jack Henry Abbott (second page) to Norman Mailer, August 29, 1978. *(Harry Ransom Center, The University of Texas at Austin)*

Eastern State Penitentiary. *(Courtesy of Eastern State Penitentiary Historic Site)*

Soledad Brothers, George Jackson funeral, 1971. *(AP Images)*

Gary Gilmore awaiting execution, 1977. *(AP Images)*

Richard Adan shortly before his death, 1981. *(Ricci Adan)*

Ricci Reyes Adan, 1981. *(Ricci Adan)*

New York City Detective William J. Majeski following Abbott's capture, 1981. *(Neal Boenzi/*New York Times*/Redux)*

Jack Henry Abbott at trial, 1982. *(AP Images)*

Norman Mailer during Abbott's manslaughter trial in 1982.
(UPI Images)

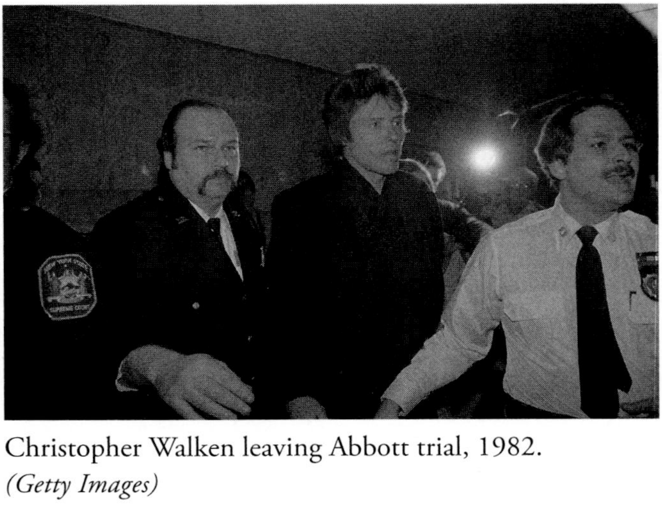

Christopher Walken leaving Abbott trial, 1982.
(Getty Images)

ern intellectual and political history, with allusions to Sartre, Lenin, Marx, Engels, Nietzsche, Kierkegaard, Stalin, and Mao. Abbott, Mailer would write in his introduction to *In the Belly of the Beast*, had a mind like no other he had ever encountered. "It speaks from the Nineteenth Century as clearly as from the Twentieth. There are moments when the voice that enters your mind is the clear descendant of Marx and Lenin untouched by any intervention of history." Abbott also ventured into literature from time to time. Here he seems to have avoided most American literature out of a hatred of the United States. (When he did get free, he planned to move to a communist country, most likely Cuba.) The "British" poet T. S. Eliot was a favorite of his in spite of his American origins. All art, he felt, had to show in some way human suffering. Here he turned to Gilmore and asked Mailer whether anyone truly had to ask themselves *why* Gilmore insisted on being executed. Abbott didn't fully understand why he killed those two men, but he did understand why he chose death over life in prison—which in Gilmore's case meant, with the indefinite suspension of capital punishment, life on death row, life without the privileges of a regular prisoner.[5]

On January 5 of the new year, Jack was still in Lompoc. He found the place relaxing, more or less, because he was a seasoned con who knew all the tricks of prison survival. Once he had "pipe-whipped" or stabbed at least half a dozen cons, the rest would stand back when he passed. But the first ten years in prison, he told Mailer, had been the worst. He lived on the verge of insanity, constantly thinking of ways either to escape or commit suicide. The only things that "saved" him were books, mainly available because of the prison reform movement of the 1970s. He read everything he could get his hands on and burned to know. It was only in the "hole" that he was denied any book but the Bible—and then only in state prison in Utah. To counter that deprivation, he often played a game with himself in which he strove to recount everything he had ever read. "I could then recite most of 'Paradise Lost' and *all* of 'The Raven,'" he extravagantly claimed. "That's not counting 20 or 30 short poems by classic Irish-English poets."[6]

9

Gilmore in Texas

Gary Mark Gilmore was born in McCamey, Texas—not much more than a crossroads near the intersection of Routes 67 and 385 in West Texas, an oil boomtown in the 1920s named after its first oilman. The town had around 2,500 inhabitants in December 1940, when Gilmore came into the world and boosted its population by one. Today it has fallen to around 1,800, with a quarter of its residents living below the poverty line. Wikipedia lists its most famous four citizens in alphabetical order, but Gilmore would have been first even without that ordering; the others are Jill Jackson, Bill Keffer, and Dan Seals. Gary's father, Frank, was a con man on the lam from the law, with his wife, Bessie, and one-year-old son in tow when she gave birth to Gary at the Burleson Hotel. They remained for six weeks. Bessie remembered the people in the hotel were "crazy" about the infant. Gary visited the town again as a teenager, having hitchhiked there with a couple of friends, all of them embarking on a life of crime. He was born to fail in so many ways, and McCamey, Texas, became the first way.

Gary wasn't even born with his real name. On the birth certificate, his first name was "Faye," which harkened back to one of his father's antecedents; his middle name was Robert; and his last name was "Coffman," an alias his father, Frank Gilmore, Sr., was using at the time. His mother Bessie, upon waking from her postnatal nap, was surprised to hear herself addressed as Mrs. Coffman. Within a few weeks, she renamed her second child Gary after Gary Cooper, "because he's going to grow up to be handsome, just like the actor."[1]

Frank Gilmore, born in 1890, was a petty criminal for the first fifty years of his life. When he started the family that produced Gary, he made a living as a scammer, coming up with schemes which, if done legally, would have probably made him as much money. Instead, he went from town to town in the West selling bogus advertising for a magazine that never appeared. Houdini-like, Frank Sr. would disappear, his confidence underscored by the legend that his grandfather had been the famed Harry Houdini (he wasn't). His criminal record began when he was twenty-four, in 1914. He served two years of hard labor in San Quentin for embezzlement in 1919.

By 1937, after taking his confidence games around the country for ten or fifteen years, marrying and deserting at least two women along the way, he met the twenty-three-year-old Bessie Brown in Salt Lake City. At the time, she was either in or about to enter into an unsuccessful marriage. By the next year, when that marriage had failed, she and Frank got together, though they did not officially marry until years later. Bessie's Mormon parents did not approve of their daughter's involvement with Frank because of his shady past and Roman Catholic affiliation—they more or less scorned the couple. As a result, the two eventually left Salt Lake City for a series of small towns, where Frank continued his swindles. The first of their four sons, Frank Gilmore, Jr., was born in 1939. Gary came along the following year.

It was while on the road in Missouri in 1942, when Gary was still a baby, that Frank abandoned his wife and first son in the middle of nowhere. While Bessie was changing Frank Jr., in a gas station bathroom, Frank took off with Gary in the backseat and did not return. Waiting until nightfall, she was directed to a place where she could call her parents to come rescue her. The next time she heard from Frank, he was jailed in Iowa for passing bad checks. Young Gary had been placed in an orphanage in Des Moines until his mother could claim him. Apparently, Frank felt that the law had gotten too close to him on the day he abandoned his wife and child. Some months later, the law caught up with him as he continued his bunko routine under different pseudonyms. Under one of them, "Harry F. Laffo," Frank was sentenced to five years in Colorado State Penitentiary. "Seeing the devastated look on his face," his fourth son writes in *Shot in the Heart* (1995), "Bessie found herself feeling more pity for him than anger. He looked like a crushed man." Frank served eighteen months and was paroled on July 3, 1943, when he returned to his family, then living in Provo, Utah, near Bessie's sister Ida and her husband Vern

Damico, who would become players in Gary Gilmore's drama in *The Executioner's Song*.[2]

Mostly through with crime, Frank nevertheless returned to his family as a changed but "mean man." He frequently whipped the two boys for the slightest infractions, especially Gary, whose more consistent misbehavior may have reminded Frank of his own past deeds as a grifter. It was only with the birth of his third son, Gaylen, in Los Angeles in 1944 that the ex-con became an affectionate father. The family continued to move around the country, finally settling in Portland, Oregon, where Frank made an honest living for the first time, publishing a magazine called *Building Code Digest*. He ultimately expanded it into other cities. He bought a house in Portland and proceeded to embark with his wife and now three children on a middle-class existence. As a father, however, he favored Gaylen over the older two boys. Except for beatings, Frank ignored his first two sons. Michael Gilmore recalled from one of his brother's reminiscences, "my father quickly formed a special love for [Gaylen]. It was as if, overnight, the novelty of the other boys wore off for him."[3] Afterward, his affection for Gaylen extended and increased for Michael Gilmore, who was born in 1951. Michael, who unofficially changed his first name to Mikal as a teenager, obviously experienced a different father from the one known to Frank Jr. and Gary.

After settling in Portland, there was a brief interlude during which the family moved back to Salt Lake City, where both Frank Jr. and Gary missed their school friends from Portland. It was during this time, his mother later recalled, that Gary began to get into trouble. Young Frank soon realized what bad company they had become acquainted with, but Gary, then eleven, fell in with those tough kids in Salt Lake City, fooling with guns and committing petty thefts. Gary's father found much of the loot Gary had hidden in the house, thoroughly whipped him, and made him return everything on the sly. When the family returned to Portland in 1952, Gary's juvenile record was still relatively clean.

But the next four years set the criminal pattern for the rest of Gary's thirty-six years on earth. Mikal Gilmore's first memory of his brother Gary was in 1955, when he saw Gary in their kitchen surrounded by the other family members. Gary had just returned from a brief stay in reform school and was fourteen. Back home the father's beatings continued. Another thing that probably motivated Frank Sr. was the memory of his own father's neglect. "I got hit less than Gary," Frank Jr. recalled, "because Gary used to really jump and yell and scream. Dad would really go to town on him then. He would go completely off his rocker, and he just wouldn't stop. He'd keep swinging and swinging and swinging, and Gary kept yelling and crying and begging him to stop, which would only make Dad hit him harder and longer." If the physical beatings didn't scar Gary for the rest of his life, the psychological ones did. Bessie Gilmore told Larry Schiller that her husband bought Gary a baseball glove when he was little, "but every time he would do one little thing, [his father] would take the glove away from him, and Gary'd go out and play ball with no mitt or glove or whatever . . . and finally Gary wouldn't take [the glove] back when his father did give it back to him . . ." According to Mikal, who visited his brother on death row in 1977, Gary told his uncle Vern on the morning of his execution, "My father was the first person I ever wanted to murder. If I could have killed him and got away with it, I would have."[4]

Back in Portland, Gary attended the Joseph Lane School, populated mainly with working-class children. He hung out with those with the most discipline problems and soon became one of the most disruptive students in the school. It was at this time that he began breaking into homes. He looked for guns and other items he could easily pawn, but he also enjoyed seeing how other people lived, prying into their private drawers and closets. In early 1954, he ran away from home. "After that," his brother Mikal sadly concludes in his book about his brother, a brother he hardly knew until Gary was on death row in 1977 except through reminiscences by one of his other brothers, "Gary's life was one long unbroken chain of trouble until the day he died." By 1955, when Gary was fifteen, he was sent to MacLaren's Reform School. (The school is still in existence and now called MacLaren School for Boys. Back then, the committed boy's parents had to pay $35 a month for room and board, today the equivalent of just over $300). It was to be the first brutalizing experience of his lifelong incarceration. On the first night at the institution, he experienced its "cum fights," when after "lights out" the teenagers would masturbate and, like monkeys, hurl gobs of semen at each other.[5]

There were beatings, humiliations, and possibly sexual assaults at the school, and after a time Gary escaped with a few others and stole a car. They were soon apprehended and returned to MacLaren's, this time to be confined in a high-security cottage, where the inmates were frequently manacled to the walls. It was Gary's first taste of solitary confinement, and he spent most of 1955 under these harsh conditions. The next year saw a pause in his bad behavior, when he was paroled in June 1956 to live with his family. There, however, he felt emotionally distant from his brothers and was also fearful of family rejection, especially by his father, who by this time seemed simply to want to be rid of him. Now in place of beatings, his father threatened Gary with a swift return to the reform school, actually calling those authorities on one or two occasions to back up his word. Under such unwelcome conditions, the boy turned back to crime and committed his first armed robbery, of a grocery store in Portland, getting away (he was never caught for this crime) with $18,000. But his earliest stint in adult jail was right around the corner. With another boy, he broke into a building, found a gun, and accidentally shot his accomplice. At the hospital, the matter was brought to the attention of the police, who already had their eye on the two boys for general mischief and petty crime. They were charged with burglary of a building, and Gary, now sixteen, was sentenced to one year in Rocky Butte, the Multnomah County jail.[6]

Serving his full sentence, Gilmore was released from Rocky Butte in May 1958, but shortly after he was out he was accused of contributing to the delinquency of a minor, a charge that also involved rape. Subsequently on the run in California and Texas from a charge of statutory rape, he was snared for one of his car thefts when he returned to Portland. This conviction in 1960 would mark yet another prison transition—this time from county jail to an institution for older teenage offenders at the Oregon State Correctional Institution in Salem. Gary's one redeeming factor was his artistic ability, and along the way to life in prison, he was let out once to enroll in an art program at a local community college, where he failed to show up. Generally, during his year at Oregon State, art did not redeem him. He served his full yearlong sentence for disciplinary offenses, including the threatening of older prisoners, perhaps an unconscious way to strike back at the father.

By the time he was released in 1961, Gary Gilmore was close to becoming "institutionalized." Prison was much of what he really knew during his first twenty years on the planet. It had toughened him beyond recall. He told his older brother that he even missed his friends in jail, and he was afraid he was going to hurt somebody, possibly his father, who had developed cancer and would die in 1962. His only profession, he confessed, was that of a criminal. The only life he now wanted to lead was that of a gangster. At the time of his father's demise, Gary was already back in the Rocky Butte jail for driving without a license. When he got out again, his behavior became more and more violent, so that even his brothers feared him. He continued to commit petty and occasionally major crimes, anticipating his pattern in Provo in 1976, before he returned to jail for committing two murders. "Every now and then," writes Mikal Gilmore, "one of Gary's crimes would land him in jail, though never more than a couple of weeks."[7]

Gary's days of freedom came to an end in 1963, shortly after the assassination of John F. Kennedy. While facing his latest charges, this time for assault and robbery, he fell into the category of the habitual criminal, giving the judge the leeway to give Gilmore a long sentence as a "danger to society." At his trial in March of 1964, he was sentenced to fifteen years at Oregon State Prison. Following an escape and a bank robbery during the years that followed, Gilmore became a federal prisoner confined to Marion federal prison. It would be from this penal institution, the nation's highest-security prison at the time, that Gary Gilmore was released in the spring of America's bicentennial year. In 1976, as the nation celebrated its first two hundred years as the world's first democracy, Gary lived out his final act, a starring role in what became *The Executioner's Song.*

By the time Gary Gilmore got his last chance at freedom, he was damaged goods many times over. Most people other than his relatives "rejected him for what he had done before," according to one of those relatives. "Everybody was always putting him down for being in prison." Even though his friends and relatives wished the best for Gary, they were soon distracted by his prison personality, which simply could not weather "no." "That's what it seemed like to me," said another of his many cousins. "He was just uptight, he's not the kind of person that would take no for an answer or take any crap. He just wanted everythin' to go his way." Gary's chances of living free naturally ran out within months, and his only legacy to speak of was an illegitimate son, unknown to this day. A young adult by the time of Gilmore's execution, "Gary Gilmore, Jr." apparently never learned—perhaps does not know to this day—that the notorious killer was his father. Only his grandmother knew of the filial connection, and she would take that secret to her grave. Bessie Gilmore hinted of this mysterious person, her grandson, but asked Schiller "that that not be put in the book."[8]

10

The Executioner's Song: Circumstance, Substance, and Reception

Most of us who are readers and writers can name one book—a novel, usually—that turned us around at an impressionable age. That book for Norman Kingsley Mailer was James T. Farrell's *Studs Lonigan*, a naturalistic trilogy published in the 1930s. At the age of sixteen or seventeen, Mailer read all three volumes and told a friend of his sister Barbara that he considered Farrell to be "the greatest American writer, and he was going to be the second greatest." The setting for Farrell's magnum opus in the mean streets of Southside Chicago resembled Mailer's teenage milieu of Crown Heights in Brooklyn. Mailer grew up in a home "cultivated" by his Jewish family, but outside that home lay a "difficult" neighborhood: "You know," he told an interviewer in 1963, "go out in the street and . . . if you didn't have any friends you get beaten up. It was as simple as that. And so," the amateur pugilist concluded, "I was always terribly alert to the outside world."[1] Reading *Studs Lonigan*, he said, "was the first truly literary experience" he had, "because the background of Studs was similar to mine . . . Until then I had never considered my life or the life of the people around me as even remotely worthy of—well, I didn't believe they could be treated as subjects for fiction. It never occurred to me. Suddenly I realized you could write about your own life."[2]

There are dozens of rough characters in *The Naked and the Dead*, tough guys from gritty neighborhoods across the United States surviving as combatants during World War II—former hoboes and unemployed factory workers, fugitives of the Great Depression who had ridden the rails through its cities of the East and the small towns of the Midwest and South. Mailer's soldiers in his first blockbuster don't reflect the wholesome image of the GI in the movie newsreels of the time; instead, they are crude and dangerous (sometimes to one another) and more resemble the trailer-camp types in *The Executioner's Song*. In writing the first novel, Mailer followed not only the example of Farrell in *Studs* but also that of another, better remembered novelist of the 1930s, John Dos Passos, whose sprawling trilogy *U.S.A.* was published about the same time as *Studs*. Like Dos Passos, really because of his example, Mailer peppered his narrative with biographical sketches of the important characters in his war novel. His "Time Machine" sections underscore the diversity of Americans called up to fight for their country. Dos Passos's train-hopping printer in *U.S.A.*, for example, is matched by Mailer's Red Valsen, "The Wandering Minstrel," whose father has been killed in a mine explosion in Montana. "Everything about him was bony and knobbed . . . In silhouette his profile consisted almost entirely of a large blob of a nose and a low-slung jaw, a combination which made his face seem boiled and angry."[3] Valsen, like Studs, could have emerged from the mean streets of either Southside Chicago or the byways of Brooklyn.

But it was Farrell who first suggested to Mailer the literary genre of determinism, who first dramatized for this Jewish writer, whose ethnic disadvantages rivaled those of the Irish, the inverse of the American Dream. Shaped by a culturally flat environment, Studs Lonigan graduates from parochial grade school to pool halls and street corners between World War I and the Depression. By this time, the Irish had finally risen from lowest rungs of society to control everything. At the center of it all was the Catholic Church, led by Irish priests who encouraged ethnic rivalries and racism. Studs's neighborhood, centered at Fifty-ninth and Prairie, is ultimately absorbed into Chicago's Black Belt, sold off block by block by Jewish real estate agents as the Irish complete construction of the stately St. Patrick's Church. The Irish clergy also condemn the University of Chicago, where Farrell had rid himself of class hatred and become a socialist. As one young member of its congregation remarks: "The Polacks and Dagoes and niggers are the same, only the niggers are the lowest."[4]

When the first volume of Farrell's trilogy appeared in 1932, the language and content were so rough that its publisher treated it the way that censors like Anthony Comstock in the late nineteenth century condemned medical volumes, along with parts of the Bible and *Leaves of Grass*. The caveat on the back cover of *Studs* stated that the novel "is issued in a special edition, the sale of which is limited to physicians, surgeons, psychologists, psychiatrists, sociologists, social workers, teachers, and other persons having a professional interest in the psychology of adolescents." When the critic Joseph Warren Beach included *Studs Lonigan* in his study of classic American fiction of the twenties and thirties, he hesitated to give the grotesque particulars of the fall of Studs and his neighborhood cronies. Indeed, he wrote that he "would not even advise one to read [the trilogy], unless one is prepared to take the high ground in which the painful facts of human experience are transformed into tragic art."[5] He even ventured to suggest that Matthew Arnold (who famously defined literature as the "best that has been thought and said") might have excluded *Studs Lonigan* from the realm of great literature.

Gary Gilmore originates from the same kind of cultural American desert that forms the background for Studs. Both subscribe to the code of the poolroom loafer or street hoodlum, to whom school is anathema. Both love beauty, but the boredom and cynicism of their ignorant lives drive them to brutal indulgence. In *The Executioner's Song*, it is true, Mailer spends most of the book on Gilmore's time between his release and execution, but implicit in his depiction of Gilmore is a background, shared with Stud Lonigan, of street toughs and school dropouts. Mailer, an amateur boxer who punched out his share of occasionally unequal opponents (e.g., Gore Vidal), adopted his own tough-guy stance in public life, which helped him imagine Gilmore's background. "Stormin' Norman" was anything but the "Nice Jewish Boy from

Brooklyn" who simply grew up to become the obnoxious "You-Know-Who" of *Advertisements for Myself.* Mailer had paid his dues in that department. His refinement mostly began at age sixteen, when he entered Harvard as a freshman. It was there that he first discovered Farrell's classic; yet it was a case of déjà vu that allowed him to put his past under a literary microscope and begin to learn about life through literature. And almost from the beginning of his own literary efforts, he had wanted to write a novel about prison. In fact, his second unpublished novel, *A Transit to Narcissus,* eventually published under that title in 1978, takes place in an insane asylum.

Mailer takes his place in American literary history as a naturalist, following the example of not only Farrell and Dos Passos but also Dreiser, who was obviously a literary hero to all three. They are not simply naturalists in the way of Émile Zola or Frank Norris, where environment damns their characters, but also psychological novelists, whose protagonists suffer from spiritual poverty. "Studs Lonigan," Farrell told the *Atlantic Monthly* at the outset of his career, "was conceived as a normal American boy of Irish Catholic extraction. The social milieu in which he lived and was educated was one of spiritual poverty. It was not, contrary to some misconceptions, a slum neighborhood."[6] In spite of the support of home and church, however, their influence breaks down, and Studs turns to the amorality of the streets.

Gary Gilmore, as Mailer knew, also came from an "intact" family—one with a father, mother, and four boys. Though a former convict and con man, Frank Gilmore, Gary's father, ultimately made an honest and fruitful living for his family. Gary's mother was loving but also showed signs of being psychotic. His father whipped his two eldest sons, and especially Gary, unmercifully when they strayed from their youthful obligations at home and school. Bessie Gilmore beat her children and once attempted to suffocate her last born.[7] It wasn't poverty that sent Gary to hell in life; it was spiritual poverty, as has been told in chapter 9. Outside of staying on the right side of the law and making a living, there were no family standards of conduct or implications for constraint. The background story of the Gilmore family is brought out formally and thoroughly in Mikal Gilmore's history of his family. Coming along late enough to miss the wrath and cruelty of his father, whose other three sons spent time in prison, Mikal Gilmore became the artist that his brother might have become if he had not been born much earlier—at the wrong time and in the wrong place.

The Gilmore household wasn't formally religious, to say the least. Frank was born a Roman Catholic, and his wife Bessie sprang from Mormon roots. Yet *The Executioner's Song* begins biblically enough. In Mailer's "True Life Novel," Gary, after being introduced, with Brenda, to the Garden of Eden setting of their grandmother's apple orchard, is described as being "rough" with his playmates at the early age of seven. The setting is Utah, where Mormon history presses down hard on the present. "A dirt road" went past their grandmother's house and "up the slope of the valley into the canyon."[8] In the neighboring towns of Orem and Provo, Utah, where Gary murdered in two successive nights, the roads leaving the city centers are described in *The Executioner's Song* as disappearing into the desert. Gary's route from Marion federal prison back to Utah, Brenda reflects as she waits for her cousin to arrive, "was practically the same route their Mormon great-grandfather took when he jumped off from Missouri with a handcart near to a hundred years ago, and pushed west with all he owned over the prairies, and the passes of the Rockies, to come to rest at Provo in the Mormon Kingdom of Deseret just fifty miles below Salt Lake."[9]

Gary, it seems, was probably already doomed, as early as the time the family moved from Salt Lake to Portland. We get this news through the memory of Brenda, who will agree to sponsor her cousin out of Marion. "Her next memory of Gary," Mailer writes, "was not until she was thirteen. Then, her mother, Ida, told her that her Aunt Bessie [Ida's sister] had called from Portland, and was in a very blue mood. Gary had been put in Reform School." It would be another twenty-five years until she met her cousin again, this time after his release from thirteen years in prison at Oregon State and Marion, "the place they built to replace Alcatraz. [Bessie] was not accustomed to thinking of her son as a dangerous criminal who could be kept only in a Maximum Security prison."[10]

As *The Executioner's Song* deals ostensibly, if not exclusively, with Gilmore's brief time out of prison before reoffending, Jack Abbott, as he nourished Mailer's narrative with valuable details about prison life while he was writing the book, must have wondered, especially after reading *The Executioner's Song*, about his own chances on the outside after an even longer period of incarceration. In fact, Abbott would walk in Gilmore's nearly exact footsteps. Though not completely "state-raised," Gilmore had been insulated from society by bad habits and the brutality of prison, effectively placing him beyond the reach of the efforts of family and friends in Utah to set him on the straight and narrow. According to Mailer's novel, he starts drinking beer after beer almost immediately. He goes AWOL from his parole officer for a time. He tries to molest Laurel, a young babysitter in the community. He becomes romantically involved with Nicole Baker Barrett, a thrice-married teenager with two children, eventually alienating her and thus setting off his killing spree. Mailer's use of the vernacular of truck drivers, motel maids, and waitresses underscores the hopelessness of Gary's plight. After leaving Steve Hudson, her third husband, Nicole had hooked up with Joe Bob Sears, "a big slow-talking fellow" she had met in church. Joe Bob imprisons Nicole in her bedroom. "He didn't lock the door, but she still couldn't leave that room. He wouldn't let her. She cried a lot. Sometimes she screamed. Sometimes she'd sit there for hours. When he came in, he'd cuff her for making noise . . . He also fucked her a lot."[11] We don't know the particulars of Abbott's brief residence in the East Village, only that he drank a lot and frequented unsavory establishments. As already noted, he did little or no writing, just as Gilmore did little or no drawing.

"Western Voices," the first half of *The Executioner's Song*, is filled with the paycheck-to-paycheck lives of prison relatives and friends—or as the original dust-jacket copy for the book states, "the moneyless side of the modern West with its pickup trucks, its trailer camps, its petty crime, and its county jails." Brenda, clearly one of the most upstanding members of her humble neighborhood, has been married four times. Her father, Vern Damico, runs a shoe repair shop and lives next door to the City Center Motel, where Gary will commit his second murder and essentially bankrupt Vern because of the shoemaker's avuncular association with a condemned killer. Nicole's family consists of a brother, Rikki, who is estranged from his wife, Sue. Nicole's father, Charley Baker, is divorced from her mother, Kathryn; though he still associates with her, he has a girlfriend named Wendy. Nicole's younger sister, April, experiences psychological problems after being gang-raped by blacks in Hawaii, where her father briefly worked for the federal government. Nicole herself was sexually molested at age seven by "Uncle Lee," a military buddy of her father's who subsequently gets killed in Vietnam. Aside from "Uncle Lee," these are people who don't commit crimes in spite of their being in many cases no more than one or two paydays away from becoming homeless. Half of Utah is Mormon; so probably half of their number are followers of or at least acknowledge the "Church." As Mormons they do not approve of the use of alcohol, much less the commission of crimes. An ex-convict such as Gilmore surely tests their commitment to helping him go straight. He is challenged from both within and without.

Gilmore's insistence on being executed for his murders quickly captures the attention of the rest of the world. Called "Eastern Voices," part two of *The Executioner's Song* brings to bear on this otherwise common criminal statistic the worlds of commerce, law, and greed. The battle over capital punishment, somewhat dormant since no one in the United States has been executed for nearly a decade, is reignited. The celebrity world takes note, leading to a bidding battle involving David Susskind, a famous television talk show host, and the singer Paul Anka, who sends Vern his shoes to repair in the hope of finding an inside track to Gilmore's story for his own commercial purposes. Eccentric characters come out of the national woodwork. An unemployed lawyer named Dennis Boas appears to defend Gary's right to die. In exchange, he wants the rights to Gilmore's story for half of the publication proceeds. We get viewpoints from all angles—death penalty friends and foes, a *National Enquirer* reporter, a representative of the ACLU in Utah, reporters both local and national who scheme to profit from the national melee. Once the story breaks nationally in *The New York Times* of November 8, 1976, and Gilmore's picture appears on the cover of *Newsweek* of November 29, there is no letting up until Gilmore's execution in January of 1977.

In this "true life novel," Mailer follows the facts both in the press and in the various testimonies, or "stories," provided by Larry Schiller, who had managed to outbid or outwit mainly Susskind and capture the rights to Gilmore's saga. *The Executioner's Song* is so faithful to the evidence, in fact, that this novel should have had an index. Yet it would be akin to indexing *Moby-Dick*, which also presents many characters (and Melville's masterpiece is surely full of facts about the whaling industry). It's what both writers bring to evidence, facts, and truth that make their works fiction. *The Executioner's Song* is full of details, in which the point—or points—of view emanate from the characters themselves instead of from a detached storyteller or novelist, who in this case remains outside the story (as perhaps it should have been since, unlike Schiller, who doesn't and thus becomes part of the story, Mailer never met Gilmore). Mailer had written "true life" works of fiction before. In fact, the subtitle for *The Armies of the Night* is *History as a Novel, The Novel as History.*

"Eastern Voices" presents an array of advocates and enemies of capital punishment, lawyers pro and con and various death penalty specialists who seek to interview Gilmore at the state prison in Draper. Crossing the stage of this national drama, played out in the newspapers and newscasts, are everybody from the prosecutor, who supports the execution, to the governor, who delays it. During the postponement, Gary and Nicole attempt a dual, or simultaneous, suicide in which Gary fails to give himself a lethal dose and Nicole is hospitalized for several weeks, never to see her lover again, except on the "other side." Both believe that their suicides would have resulted in immediate reincarnation, but in between Gary's return to prison and his execution, Nicole, too, may have had her own doubts because, Mailer writes, she manages to have sex with at least three other men, including the manager of a grocery store in Springville who gives her cash for food stamps.

During the first phase of Gilmore's incarceration, he is held in a city jail, where his cellmate, Gibbs ("Geebs"), turns out to be a police informer. After Gary is moved to Draper, Gibbs sends him cartoons and jokes in the press about his approaching execution.

One item is a sketch of Gilmore lying in a hospital bed after his suicide attempt. "The nurse was saying, 'Mr. Gilmore wake up. It's time for your shot.' At the foot of the hospital bed was a five-man firing squad." In another example of the gallows humor that punctuates part two, a doctor tells the patient that he "can leave the hospital and return to Death Row if he continues to improve." As he finally leaves his cell for the execution, he shocks one of his lawyers, Bob Moody, by telling him not to forget to bring his bulletproof vest.[12] As the comic novelist and critic David Lodge observed in his *TLS* review of January 11, 1980, a presence of mind at a time like that "inevitably make[s] one wonder why a man capable of such wit and acumen came to be in a condemned cell at all."

By page 887, we come to the actual execution. The scenes that follow are so vivid and factual that one must indeed wonder about which tense to use in the description in this "true life novel"—to relate Gilmore's facts and Mailer's "nonfiction." Gary invites his max of five people: Nicole (who after the suicide attempt is not allowed to attend); Vern Damico (who manages Gary's income from various sources dealing with the story); his lawyers, Ron Stanger and Bob Moody; and Larry Schiller. In his last letter to her, Gary tells Nicole that a place will be saved in her honor, adding one last suggestion that she join him in death sooner rather than later: "*Baby I've been avoiding something but I'll come to it right now. If you choose to join me or if you choose to wait—it is your choice.*"[13]

On the eve of Gary's execution, while more than three hundred members of the international press wait in the parking lot outside the execution chamber, Gary's death vigil turns into a party of family and close friends. Ever the host, he refuses any food, saying he hopes that everybody was enjoying his last meal. When Johnny Cash calls, he asks the "outlaw" singer of "Folsom Prison Blues," "Are you the real Johnny Cash?" Hearing the affirmative, he "hollered back, 'Well, this is the real Gary Gilmore.'"[14] Fame is Gary's, however fleeting. By nearly 8:00 A.M. Mountain Time on January 17, 1977, he is moved to the execution area. There is still a chance the Supreme Court will order a stay, but that possibility disappears at three minutes after eight. With the execution coming after a ten-year drought on the use of the death penalty, the prison has to use its cannery as the safest place for an execution by firing squad. "The seat of execution," Mailer writes, "was no more than a little old office chair, and behind it was an old filthy mattress backed up by sandbags and the stone wall of the cannery."[15] Each witness on Gary's guest list comes up to shake hands with the condemned. Once Gary mouths the words that rang around the world ("Let's do it"), three or four men place a hood over his head and add a waist and head strap. A doctor pins a white circle on Gilmore's dark shirt, after which he neatly steps back from the intended target. Rifle barrels project through slits of the blind, and witnesses are shocked to see how close the blind is to the victim. Floodlights illuminate the target. Even though every bullet enters Gilmore's heart, he doesn't die immediately. It takes, however, no more than twenty seconds, when the exit wounds spurt streamlets of blood in Gilmore's back, some of which stain the raiment of the attending clergyman, Father Meersman. As the witnesses are ordered to leave the execution site, one of them (Schiller) murmurs that there "aren't going to be less murders" because of Gary's execution.[16]

This tale of crime and punishment concludes with Gary's uncle and mother, both left devastated by the execution and the life that led up to it. The rest of 1977 is not a good year for Uncle Vern. His "leg was so bad he needed another operation, but he had no money. Because he could not stand on his feet for a full day, he had to sell his store, and then there were lawsuits against Gary's estate," contesting for the money Schiller had paid Gilmore for his story. Then his wife suffered a stroke; she would die in the next decade while Vern, who lived into the twenty-first century, died at the age of ninety. His sister-in-law, Bessie, is last seen living out her final years in a run-down trailer in Oregon, occasionally harassed by threatening letters and people asking permission to include Gary in songs: "She would just sit there. If a car came at night, came into the trailer park, drove around and slowed up, if it stopped, she knew somebody out there in that car was thinking that she was alone by the window." But she has nothing to lose and is not afraid: "If they want to shoot me, I have the same kind of guts Gary has. Let them come."[17]

While admiring Mailer's achievement in *The Executioner's Song*, more than a few readers and at least one reviewer wondered whether the word "tragic," as it was employed and implied in the dust-jacket summary was deserved, whether Gilmore wasn't just a punk who didn't deserve all the attention he received. Christopher

Lehmann-Haupt, who wrote the weekday *New York Times* review of the book on September 24, 1979, agreed, saying that Gilmore "never for a moment showed the slightest insight as to why he had committed the murders. As for his affair with Nicole Baker, which the dust jacket of the book suggests we may regard as 'tragic': she strikes one on the whole as being little more than a spaced-out drifter not even capable of looking after her own children."

John Cheever, the famed short-story writer ("Chekhov of the Suburbs") agreed. Characterizing the suburbs of Salt Lake City as a "nomadic crossroads of the Midwest" where Gary "blows out the brains of [two] exceptionally intelligent, purposeful, and loving young husband[s]," he noted ironically in the *Chicago Tribune* of October 7, 1979, that Nicole's suicide note mentioned that she had a pearl ring "in hock in the bowling alley in Springville," which she would like "for someone to get it and give it to my little sister April L. Baker." Cheever had just won the Pulitzer Prize for his collection of short stories, the same prize Mailer would win for *The Executioner's Song* in 1980.

Mailer must have cherished the review nearly as much as he did the one by Joan Didion. Writing in the Sunday *New York Times Book Review* for October 7, 1979, Didion, who, as one of the masters of the new journalism, or creative nonfiction, had been asked by Schiller to write the book before he asked Mailer, concluded her admiring essay by saying, "This is an absolutely astonishing book." Instead of seeing *The Executioner's Song* as the fulfillment of a promise made long ago with *The Naked and the Dead*, Didion expresses her admiration not simply for such non-fiction imaginative masterpieces as *The Armies of the Night* (1968) but also for fiction that met with mixed literary success such as *The Deer Park* (1955), *An American Dream* (1965), and *Why Are We in Vietnam?* (1967). She sees *The Executioner's Song* as yet another in the series of the "big book" or "Great American Novel." Yet in doing so, Didion acknowledged that Mailer kept himself and his ego out of the book, relying instead on Schiller's facts. What he didn't keep out, of course, was his ingenious handling of those facts, writing "a thousand-page novel in a meticulously limited vocabulary and a voice as flat as the horizon" in Utah. His "deliberately featureless" dialogue slides "over the mind like conversations at K-Mart." No one else (including herself, apparently) "could have dared this book," whose first half speaks of the "vast emptiness" of the western experience, with its beer joints and barbecue pits, its trailer parks and pickup trucks. Discussing both the West and East of the novel's structure, she finds that the American wasteland extends to the voices of both—"a nihilism antithetical not only to literature but to most other forms of human endeavor, a dread so close to zero that human voices fade out," stifled in Gilmore's case by a shot in the heart, in an execution harking back to frontier days.

Cheever further articulated the anti–capital punishment message that runs through Mailer's "true life" novel. "The detonative force [of Gilmore's decision to force his execution]," Cheever wrote, "was, of course, inestimable, based on the unconscionable obscenity of a public execution at this point in our history." He also bemoaned the shame of entertainment journalism: "The entertainment values of a public execution are bid for by David Susskind and Larry Schiller, who has already exploited Susan Atkins' life and Jack Ruby's last interview. The hard core of this merchandise is a thousand ardent love letters and the taped interviews the condemned man has agreed [to make public]." The entire story from its private beginning to its public end sheds a bad light, he concluded, on our judiciary, our penitential system, and the journalistic enterprise to be first with the "news."

The novelist Diane Johnson picked up the cudgel against Schiller in *The New York Review of Books* of December 6, 1979. "Once you are in the mind of Schiller," she wrote, "it becomes obvious why Mailer has kept himself out of the narrative. This account of the exploitation of the poor convict and his relatives is so appalling that the author of the end product—the book you are reading—must seem to be innocent of it, must seem not to be writing it at all . . . It is the 'carrion bird' Schiller who must seem the bad guy, and Mailer does such a job on him that you would suppose they are now estranged." Mailer complained about the review to editor Robert Silvers, and Johnson subsequently published a "Correction and Clarification" (February 21, 1980), pointing out that Mailer had not agreed to write the book until after Gilmore's execution, thereby putting some distance between the author and the "carrion bird."[18]

Several reviewers held their nose when discussing Schiller's role in the novel as well as his background in what was termed "checkbook journalism." In *The Hollywood Reporter* of December 7, 1979, Germaine Greer referred to Schiller as a "superghoul." In complaining about that review, too, Mailer told the editor that

Schiller "never took the money and ran. He stayed close to all of the job and kept working with indefatigable energy, doing half the interviews and clearing paths for me in a thousand ways . . . so that I could be free to do the best writing I was capable of."[19]

With no love lost because of Mailer's attack on Kate Millett's *Sexual Politics* (1970), in *The Prisoner of Sex* (1971) superfeminist Greer opined that the best writing to be found in *The Executioner's Song* lay in the condemned man's love letters to Nicole. Yet another writer of large reputation, Larry McMurtry, thought the book the "masterpiece" Mailer had been looking for ever since *The Naked and the Dead*. "The nobility of the book," McMurtry wrote in the *New West* of October 22, 1979, "resides in the sympathy and insight with which Mailer penetrates and reconstructs the pattern and nuance" of the "many people bound up with Gilmore's actions." He admired Mailer's "fidelity to idiom and intonation" and suggested that the novel's best parts called to mind "the compassionate realism of Dreiser and Farrell." Frank McConnell, in *The New Republic* of October 27, concurred with McMurtry's praise, calling *The Executioner's Song* a perfect parable of winning and losing and of "existential nakedness." McConnell expressed appreciation for the cutting and shaping of preexisting material—the real work in the making of a historical novel. John Garvey, of *Commonweal* (March 14, 1980), also thought the novel was the best Mailer had written in many years.

Joan Didion's review has been generally considered Mailer's best for *The Executioner's Song*, but David Lodge (*TLS*, January 4, 1980) puts his finger on Mailer's accomplishment in mastering the classic realistic novel, "which has been so assiduously deconstructed and to an extent discredited by contemporary criticism." Lodge, a literary critic best known for satirizing academe in a campus trilogy of novels, knows of what he speaks. The targets of such novels as *Changing Places* (1975) and *Small World* (1984), for example, were the deconstructionists and relativists in both the United States and Britain who undercut the traditional premises for representing reality. Yet with the nonfiction novel the author regains his hold on actual reality because "his story is based entirely on verifiable sources" (e.g., Schiller's tape recordings, Gilmore's love letters, newspaper accounts, and prison records). Although not first in doing what Dreiser did in *An American Tragedy* or what Capote did in *In Cold Blood*, Mailer, Lodge asserts, treads that thin line between fact and fiction, requiring the highest of professional skill and self-discipline. "There is a nice moment in *The Armies of the Night*," Lodge concludes, "when Robert Lowell says, a shade patronizing to Mailer, 'I really think you are the best journalist in America,' and Mailer replies, 'Well, Cal . . . there are days when I think of myself as the best writer in America.' *The Executioner's Song* does not weaken this claim."

Robert F. Lucid, the University of Pennsylvania professor who at the time was Mailer's designated authorized biographer, summed up his subject's achievement in *The Philadelphia Inquirer* of October 21, 1979. Noting, as others had, that Mailer keeps himself out of the story—no "posing, posturing, upstaging everyone else"—he points out significantly that Mailer also did not follow his usual practice, articulated in "The White Negro," of making a hero out of an outlaw. Gilmore, he insisted, is the "organizing presence in the narrative," a focal point rather than a hero, "a center around which Mailer builds a world." And that world is the culture of the west, specifically the remote Mormon outpost of Utah. And the heroes of it are not Gilmore but the people or class from which he sprang. "Not since *The Grapes of Wrath* or, perhaps, *Let Us Now Praise Famous Men*," Lucid writes, "has there been an American book that so discovered the voices and, therefore, the existence of a lost world in our culture." Gilmore can no longer function among them after so many years as a prisoner. In a prophetic, almost haunting nod to Gilmore's legacy in the embodiment of Abbott, Lucid remarks that everything he does on the outside "reveals him for what he pathetically is: a gifted human being totally unsuited to live outside of a cage."

11

Utah State

When Kennedy was murdered on November 22, 1963, and twenty-two-year-old Gary Mark Gilmore was about to live out his last days of freedom for the next twelve years, Jack Henry Abbott was already behind bars, serving his time at that juncture in solitary confinement in the Utah State Prison at "Point of the Mountain." He recalled that when the prisoners in the hole heard the news of the assassination, they cheered. He was nineteen years old and had already done more than a year's time in adult prison, serving because of discipline infractions more than the "zero" of his zero-to-five-year prison sentence for hot checks. Had Gilmore remained in that Iowa orphanage back in 1942 and been adopted by the right family, he might have gone straight, perhaps have already graduated from college in 1963, having gone, perhaps, to Oregon State University to study art instead of Oregon State Prison to study crime. Abbott's mother gave birth to six children, all or most of them by different fathers. Jack and his half-sister were kept, while the other four were put up for adoption. One wonders, too, about their fates. Surely, they fared better than Jack, perhaps better than Frances Amador, who lived in near poverty and whose husband also served time in prison. If Jack, with his high IQ, had gotten away with his other four half siblings, he might have been majoring in philosophy or English and approaching his junior year at Utah State in the wake of the presidential assassination. One bad turn, one unfortunate circumstance setting off a chain reaction of unfortunate circumstances, changed the lives of both Gilmore and Abbott, condemning them to a life behind bars.

So Jack went to the other state institution, too, and by 1979 had earned that college education on his own, not only the equivalent bachelor's degree but also the postgraduate one of a Ph.D. in philosophy, literature, and political science, majoring in the "School of Karl Marx" and "hard knocks." He had served time in Leavenworth, Springfield, Atlanta, McNeil Island, Butner, and Marion, besides Utah State at "Point of the Mountain." He had received his "doctorate at Leavenworth" by the early 1970s. By 1978 he was Fyodor Dostoyevsky, pumping out his own "notes from the underground" to Mailer, whose first draft of *The Executioner's Song* in December 1978 had been revised for the publisher by April of the following year.

"How good is it?" he mused to Abbott in a letter of April 4, "I don't know, but I think it's fairly good at the worst, and very flat in style, for which I worked." There was something in Gilmore's story that got to him, he told Abbott. "I felt I might provide the datum for Americans." As Joan Didion would write in her review, Mailer wrote the novel in the vernacular of Utah underclass that made up Gary's circle of relatives and friends. Mailer told Abbott that there was in his book very little about the twelve years

Gilmore had served in prison before his disastrous release, but there were echoes of his prison days, and "part of my understanding of that experience has come from your letters."

Even though *The Executioner's Song* was finished, Mailer still hoped that he and Jack would continue to correspond. He admitted to Abbott that he had once been a Marxist himself but had moderated in his radical leanings, finding Marxism in his intellectual maturity somewhat arid. Yet he was sure that there was still a "correspondence" between Abbott and himself. He would not, he promised, ever sit in judgment of Abbott for being a Marxist, because "the conditions of your existence have been so incredibly harsh." No "Zionist with a hard-on," he couldn't, however, completely sympathize with Jack's admiration of the Soviet Union, where anti-Semitism was both pervasive and toxic. "Just as I don't know what it is to be a convict," he concluded, "you the fuck don't know what it is to be a Jew."[1]

In subsequent letters, the topic turned to how Mailer could help Abbott get his parole, having done the same for Eldridge Cleaver years before. By this time the author of *Soul on Ice* had returned from exile and become a conservative and a preacher, often hobnobbing with Republicans—certainly no role model for Jack. But there it was. Mailer's support had definitely been a contributing factor in Cleaver's release, after which he joined the Black Panthers and became involved in the wounding of two police officers, thus necessitating his flight to Cuba and Algeria. Would something of this sort happen with Jack Henry Abbott on the outside? Mailer must have considered the possibility, but then put the matter aside, probably because he didn't think Jack would be released anytime soon. Indeed, hardly anyone involved in helping him to his 1981 parole did.

In July 1979 Abbott was transferred from Lompoc to Marion because of a hunger strike at Lompoc, coincidentally just missing a five-day hunger strike at Marion that would lead in future years to more violent rioting and the killing of two guards. Ultimately, Marion's worst offenders were moved to the supermax in Florence. Even though Abbott had missed the strike, he was fighting charges of helping to incite a riot. At the same time, there were plans afoot for Mailer to visit Abbott in prison for the first time since they had begun to correspond. He hoped to present him with a copy of *The Executioner's Song*. Having already perused the first of three *Playboy* excerpts of the novel, Abbott told Mailer, "I can tell that you were very thorough. You got Provo (the Mormons) down pat." He had no idea, he added, that Gilmore was so "goofy," associating with a con who allegedly performed fellatio on himself and using his artistic talent to tattoo on the back of the neck of an inmate who trusted him "a real skinny little dick . . . and peanut-sized balls" instead of the rosebud he had requested.[2]

Mailer was frustrated several times in his efforts to visit Jack at Marion, barred either because he wasn't a relative or hadn't known the prisoner before his incarceration, or because they were seen as engaging in an illegal business relationship merely because Abbott was a prisoner.[3] According to biographer J. Michael Lennon, he and his brother Peter drove Mailer the fifteen miles from the airport in Carbondale, Illinois, to the prison. His brother recalled that it "was a half hour drive through a dense, leafless forest to the isolated maximum security Marion Federal Penitentiary." According to another source, the prison looked more like an airport than a prison because of the "tinted glass and clean lines of the cast-concrete gun towers." Before leaving the two brothers in their car to enter the lockup, "Norman remarked that everything, the sky, landscape, razor wire and walls were very gray and, in fact, colorless."[4]

Lennon dates the visit November 3, 1979, but it may have taken place in October. For in reading *The Executioner's Song* Jack compared the experience to "the same feeling of unreality I had when we visited." This letter is dated October 29.

He apologized to Mailer for seeming shy during the visit. "It is just that I've heard of you all my life and admired your work . . . I'm afraid I appeared rude . . . I never let you finish telling me Camus's position on capital punishment. Also when I said I'd stay in segregation, it is because in prison it is the only place I have the time to write." The two men hit it off in spite of the strict visiting conditions. Afterward, Mailer told the Lennon brothers that he thought Jack deserved a chance at freedom.

Jack read the 1,056-page book in eight days, between October 28 and November 5, 1979. He sent Mailer fifty-six pages of notes on it! Mailer had tried unsuccessfully to leave Abbott a copy of his book during his visit. Once a copy was sent to Marion, the guards would allow Jack only to look at its dust jacket through bars. The copy was finally handed over to him after he came off a hunger strike in protest against being deprived of his property. After he finished reading the book, he said in a letter of November 6, he put it and his notes aside and got drunk. He thought that *The Executioner's Song* was Mailer's best book to date, citing innovative craftsmanship and its masterful presentation of detail. What he did not praise was Mailer's characterization of Gilmore's situation. In fact, he said, there wasn't really any criticism of anyone in the book, except Gary. "Throughout the book the entire burden of the universe is placed on his poor, mortal shoulders." In a fictional novel, he added, it would make an interesting theme for fictional characters, but in a "real-life" novel, he said, somewhat enigmatically, "it is a kind of fraud of the spirit."[5] It is true that in *The Executioner's Song*, Gilmore's approaching doom becomes increasingly and abundantly clear as soon as his plane lands in Salt Lake. He is a complete stranger in the free world, not at all ready for its liberties and obligations. He breaks the rules at once and soon gets into trouble that leads to more trouble and ultimately to the tragic killings. But what to Mailer looks like the bungling of second chances looks to Abbott like fate—fate arranged by social circumstances begun in McCamey, Texas, and indeed generations before, traceable at least back to Frank Gilmore and Frank Gilmore's father, Gary's grandfather, whom, of course, he never met—indeed, never *had* to meet to "know" him genetically.

Mailer was following the American naturalistic tradition of Theodore Dreiser's *An American Tragedy*, but, unlike Dreiser, Mailer growing up never personally experienced the social deprivation that underscores a deterministic story about an indigent child or a "state-raised convict."

Dreiser published *An American Tragedy* in 1925, which, like *The Executioner's Song,* was a bestselling novel about the derailing of the American Dream that equates money with happiness. Dreiser's novel influenced *The Executioner's Song* in a number of ways, principally in its basing of a "true-life novel" on an actual criminal case. In Dreiser's case, the basis for his "true-life novel" was the story of Chester Gillette, who, in 1906, trapped between a pregnant girlfriend and a rich woman who combines the lure of sex and money, murders the poor lover in order to marry the rich one. Caught and convicted in a highly publicized trial, Gillette was executed in 1908 at Auburn State Prison in New York. Dreiser's original title for *An American Tragedy* was "Mirage."

When Jack Abbott went on trial for killing Richard Adan, he used as his main defense the fact that he was a "state-raised convict," therefore blaming the prison system for bringing him up bad. But behind the argument and certainly at its base lay the idea that society as a whole was to blame for his imbalanced combination of "duty and desire," what Dreiser, who dabbled in pseudoscience at the turn of the twentieth century, called "chemism." The term referred to the ability, or lack thereof, to juggle social responsibilities with natural tendencies or temptations. If Jack had been brought up as Norman Mailer had been, in an intact home (in spite of Barney Mailer's gambling problem), he probably wouldn't have entered foster homes, reform schools, and prison; perhaps, given his high IQ, he would have even gone to Harvard, as Mailer did. If Gary Gilmore had remained in that Iowa orphanage and been adopted by loving parents, he too may have had a shot at the American Dream instead of a shot in the heart. Mailer tried his best to empathize with the killer Gary Gilmore. In the novel, Gilmore is seen as witty and courageous in the face of his execution. Even his alleged last words ("Let's do it") were a classic example of gallows humor. But in addition to never having shared Gilmore's fateful beginning, Mailer had, with the exception of the stabbing of his second wife, never been seriously on the other side of the law. Abbott, who had a similarly fated beginning in life and who also lacked proper role models as a youth, knew something about Gilmore that Mailer would never know, or at least would never be able to fully embrace.

12

A Light at the End of the Tunnel

Mailer's inability to fully empathize with Gary Gil-more's plight is precisely why *The Executioner's Song* became his masterpiece. Perhaps the crime was simply too brutal and cold-blooded—shooting to death two helpless men on successive nights. He therefore refrained—really for the first time in his literary life—from putting himself into the picture. He told Abbott that in every other book he had written, he had tried to *teach* something about the world and its dangers. His identity theme as a secularized American Jew was the potential oppression of the state. We see that in his very first novel, in which the power-hungry Colonel Edward Cummings in *The Naked and the Dead* is a crypto-fascist, one of those who aspire to rule the roost after World War II. We see it in *The Fight*, the work that closely precedes *The Executioner's Song*, where the boxing match between Muhammad Ali and George Foreman in Zaire is nearly upstaged by the oppression of President Mobutu, a dictator who is responsible, among so many other crimes, for the hundreds of corpses beneath the giant stadium in which the fight will take place. It is the Belgian Congo all over again, the one that became the setting for Joseph

Conrad's *The Heart of Darkness* (1889). It is the same human cauldron stirred by King Leopold II of Belgium in the nineteenth century—recycled into the twentieth. But with the book that followed, Mailer didn't try to import any of these arguments. If there is an argument against capital punishment in *The Executioner's Song*, it is countered by the horror of the crimes Gilmore committed and the hypocrisy of the forces opposed to the death penalty that rally to prevent the execution—the same liberals, Mailer allows Gilmore to say, who support abortion.

Just as Mailer knew relatively little about prison life, Jack knew little about life outside prison. He was at his literary worst when writing fiction about life in the "free world," drafts of plays that he sent to Mailer, who had suggested that he try to focus on something other than prison life. But everything Jack knew came from books, written with words that in many cases he didn't even know how to pronounce or had never heard spoken. Mailer sent him a number of plays as well as other material for study. "The books arrived yesterday," he told Norman on February 16, 1980—plays by Tennessee Williams, George Bernard Shaw, Arthur Miller, Anton Chekhov, and Sean O'Casey. One of Jack's attempted dramas was entitled, not surprisingly, "The Hole." "There were always at least two stages in the hole in any prison," he had earlier told Mailer, on November 25, 1979. "First, the regular hole for men who can't be controlled in the main population. The other 'part' of the hole is for men who combined with the first quality, cannot be controlled anywhere . . . The play is about a man, how it is [that] he gets there." Ultimately, he would complete and publish a play—after he had been released from and then returned to prison—about his unfortunate encounter with Richard Adan.

While briefly out of prison in 1981, he did little or no writing. Like Gilmore, the artist in him came alive only behind bars. Prison had become his natural environment after so many years in lockup. He spoke of the revolving door of prisoners he had observed all his jailed life: "Almost every one of them . . . feels relieved to be back. They need shaves and showers; they are gaunt, starved-looking when they come in from the outside. Within a week they are rosy-cheeked; starched-and-pressed; talking to everyone . . . They fit in prison. This is where they belong."[1]

When Norman Mailer won the Pulitzer Prize in the spring of 1980, Abbott thought it would boost his own chances for an early state parole once he was transferred from Marion to Utah. The move was scheduled for June 26, 1980. Mailer had already written his letter in support of Abbott's parole from his state prison sentence. Abbott feared only that Marion might instead ship him off to Folsom Prison instead of to Draper on "the prisoner-exchange agreement with California." Since he had been on a hunger strike at Marion (and was down to 114 pounds when he wrote Mailer about his concern), they might try to punish him further before allowing any federal parole. This didn't happen. For one thing, Jack's potential as an author was soon to be confirmed and advertised by the pieces he placed in *The New York Review of Books* of June 26 and October 9; there, he would also establish himself as an authority of prison abuse. "What the fuck the east-coast WASP mob of the New York Review of Books sees in me is fascinating," he exclaimed to Mailer in May, 1980, on the acceptance of "In Prison," as *In the Belly of the Beast* was about to be edited at Random House. His latest play, this one to be called "The Beast," probably became the seed for his book title, since it was about a "state-raised convict" like himself. He thought that "the mass phenomenon" was "as recent as the 1950s in America."[2]

Jack learned in late summer that, once he was released from Marion, he would possibly have to serve only one more year in Draper; in fact, it would be even less time than that. With Mailer's encouragement, he was rewriting the material of the lost letters and had recomposed about 45,000 words, which he sent to Random House on August of 1980.[3] He reread all the available letters and marked "the best passages," he told Mailer on August 14, 1980. "Then I thought on it and I comprehended the whole under a number of themes that emerged from the various subjects in the letters . . . I first put in passages that deal with prison generally and prison punishment in particular." His editor was Erroll McDonald, a 1975 graduate of Yale who visited Jack at Marion after working on the reconstructed letters. McDonald had first proposed the book after reading Jack's articles in *The New York Review of Books*. By the next month, Abbott had already received half of his $12,500 royalty advance.

"Well, another year," Abbott wrote Mailer on New Year's Day 1981. "I hope this one finally sees me free." (If he could only have known what freedom had in store for him.) At most, he thought he had another eighteen months in prison. Once out and a published author, he vowed not to become "a professional ex-convict." His "sights" were on "literature" now. Yet in the very next paragraph, he turned back to the subject of prison, where it was a "virtue to be illiterate"—where the most nagging question was whether you'd be able to kill preemptively in order to survive. "One anguishes and despairs that he may not be able to bring himself to a cold-blooded act of premeditated murder *with a knife*."

By the middle of January, Abbott was taken from Marion and placed in a federal jail in Chicago before being sent back to Utah. Held in isolation for about a week, he enjoyed his view of the streets of the city eleven stories below. Able to take along some of the books Mailer had sent him, he was reading Matthew Arnold's "Dover Beach" and raving about it. "What a fine poet!" he exclaimed, possibly after Arnold's allegorical description of the sea as "the turbid ebb and flow / Of human misery." He noted Arnold's obvious influence on T. S. Eliot, one of Abbott's favorite poets. He wondered whether Mailer took his title from the work for *The Armies of the Night*, from the line ending, "where ignorant armies clash by night." He was reading Chaucer, "The Monk's Tale," actually rereading *The Canterbury Tales* from twenty years earlier. Dylan Thomas's "Fern Hill" left him "shaking like a tuning-fork." Abbott, in transit from prison to prison, was in heaven.[4]

When he arrived back at Utah State Prison in the first week of February, however, he was not so ecstatic. A caseworker at Draper threatened to cut off correspondence between Abbott and Mailer (Jack's lifeblood) because it was assumed that the two had a "business relationship" with each other. Since Mailer was a "professional writer," it followed that he was buying Jack's letters. Abbott asked Mailer to speak to the warden about the problem as well as about his sponsorship of Jack's pending parole, which now looked further away than before. "I'll be going before the Parole Board in 2 or 3 months now," he wrote on February 10, 1981. "If they do not set a parole date, I don't know what I'll do. It's just too much anymore." The prison officials had also "ripped off" his personal property mailed to him from Marion. "These Mormons have certain cultural characteristics that, in dealing with a non-Mormon *prisoner*, are the equivalent of creating personality clashes of a violent nature." If he didn't get out, he said, he'd die in there.

That winter, Mailer published a piece on the death penalty in *Parade* magazine. It could have been a piece he had once considered placing at the end of *The Executioner's Song*. "Until Dead: Thoughts on Capital Punishment" discussed the pros and cons of the issue—first, the specious claim that it deters crime and then the crimes "that make one sick with rage." He concluded that society "living amid the blank walls of technology, we require . . . the official bloodbath [of execution] to restore ourselves to the idea that society is not only reasonable, but godlike."[5] Jack felt that Mailer had been too, too easy on "the police, judges, and prosecutors." He found ironic the fact that he was sitting in a cell in maximum security, which had previously served as death row when he was in Draper ten years before. The critique morphed back into the same lament about his chances for an early parole, though this time one with a certain sardonic tone to it. "There is still no hope in sight that I will be paroled anytime soon, and I've been in prison now for *over* eighteen years. Am I so frightening? (Don't answer that!)." In an allusion to Eliot's poem "The Love Song of J. Alfred Prufrock," he closed, "I'm already 'wearing the bottoms of my trousers rolled.'"[6]

Back at Draper, his sister was able to visit him again, after an absence of almost ten years, and did so regularly. While at Marion and elsewhere in the federal maze, he had gone nearly a decade without a visit from her. She was the only one of his relatives he wanted to see. As noted earlier, he was uneasy seeing her with Ben Amador, her husband. And he regarded the interests of his nieces and nephews as artificial and forced. He had also recovered his property, or books, sent from Marion—Baudelaire's *Fleurs du mal*, the complete works of Rimbaud, Kierkegaard's "Silentio" books—*Fear and Trembling, The Sickness unto Death*. This last work by Kierkegaard is about despair, which occurs for the Christian from a misalignment with God. For Abbott, whose only "religion" at the time was Marxism, his sense of despair resonated more with his living death in prison, where recidivism was generational. Everywhere he looked within the prison, he saw the sons of men who were themselves youngsters when he first came to Draper at the age of eighteen. "Their fathers no longer come to prison and live—for the most part—ordinary lives outside. I shit you not." He'd seen as many as eight sons of men with whom he had first served. "I even know some of their mothers!" he exclaimed. "It is spooky for me to see the ghosts of so long ago still haunting this place in the unconscious mannerisms and personalities of men no longer of this prison world. And I remain, to live with all this all over again!"[7]

By March 1981 he was correcting the galleys to his first book. He had reiterated in it his positive views of the Communist superpowers, China and Russia, as well as the Third World movement. Later, at the last moment, prior to publication but after bound galleys had been distributed to book reviewers, he removed, to the astonishment of his publisher, approximately 1,500 words of the printed text that described his claim that he had been tortured at Marion. It was too dangerous, as it might screw up his parole or even lead to a hit on him once outside. He had also been warned by the Marion officials before his release, he said, that if he included anything in his book about the torture incident at Marion, his "confession" would be used to prosecute him on trumped-up charges and return him to prison. Because the excision was made after the printing of advance reading copies, therefore, reviewers saw material the public never read.

He also edited Mailer's foreword, removing the reference to his killing of Christensen in 1967, something not included in the book proper, even though he was convicted of the crime. For his own safety, he also omitted any reference to the Aryan Brotherhood in prison. With *In the Belly of the Beast,* he wanted to put prison behind him, laying it all out once and for all, so as to get on with his life outside prison. "I'm even having all my tattoos removed (I only have 2 or 3 that were put in when I was 11 or 12), and I'm changing my name," he told Mailer on March 23, 1981. "I'll write under Abbott but I won't live under that name. Nor, under my new name, will I even admit to have been in prison. I'm done with it."

His next date with the parole board was April 8. Everything looked positive. They had Mailer's promise that he would employ Jack as his literary assistant at $150 a month. The work would involve research for *Ancient Evenings*. He had a letter of support from Robert Silvers, of *The New York Review of Books*. Larry Schiller had visited him. The producer was in Salt Lake City arranging permission to use the old county jail for his 1982 film on Gilmore, based on *The Executioner's Song*. "That will help my parole 'indirectly,'" Abbott told Mailer, "to have me here along with outsiders interested in the Gilmore story." The identification with Gilmore was already forming. Abbott would become Gilmore unbound, reborn, or back from the grave four years after his execution in the same prison from which Jack was about to be released.

Painful evidence of Abbott's longevity in prison manifested itself in the fact that one of the members of the Utah parole board had been a young caseworker at Draper when Abbott escaped in 1971. "He thinks I do not remember him, but I do." Back then he had been sympathetic toward Jack, "but there was nothing he could do." He would need that friendly face because Marion provided nothing but negatives in the parole hearing—three pages "with recitation of my sins with no favorable recommendations." Nevertheless, there was absolutely no question that Abbott had served enough time in prison for crimes already committed; the question was whether he could adjust, or readjust, to society—that he might remain angry at society for sending him to prison for so long that he might, when cornered, resort to violence on the outside.[8]

As it turned out, the Utah state law on which he had been convicted and sentenced in 1971 had changed retroactively in terms of the allowable maximum sentence, making his release from Draper a matter of months instead of years. He had been transferred from Marion to Draper in April, and his federal parole was now scheduled to begin on August 26, 1981, and run until 1986. Because federal law required that prisoners slated for release spend at least ninety days in a halfway house before the commencement of the actual parole, Jack was scheduled to be released from Draper on May 26 but that wasn't for more than another week. He left jail not only with his state time "served" but also with the news, he told Mailer, that Random House had already received advance orders for nine thousand copies of *In the Belly of the Beast*, still today considered one of the most compelling prison narratives in America. He was coming out of prison as a celebrity author. Highly positive reviews of his book had already appeared, weeks before the actual publication. *The Washington Post* found his prose "remarkable." The *Los Angeles Times* thought it "was touched with greatness."[9]

"I just told the board I was raised in a cage," he told Mailer in reference to his final federal parole hearing, as the day of his actual release approached. Earlier, on April 9, 1981, he told of a dream about being released. The "sweats and jitters" in it had stunned him into euphoria: "*I am on the streets*!!! I can't *believe* it! . . . I'm scared to death! I don't know how to take care of myself. I don't even know the *questions* to ask . . . I'll have to feed myself . . . It has never occurred to me in my remembered life that I had to decide what I was going to eat for dinner. I don't know how to think in those terms . . . I can't *imagine* myself shopping for anything."

He was emerging from a prison life of sensory deprivation. It would almost be like coming out of the darkness of solitary confinement after a long stretch. His plan, he said, was to get out of the state of Utah as soon as possible. But first he wanted to go with his sister and visit the grave sites of his mother (whose funeral prison officials had not allowed her eighteen-year-old son to attend) and his maternal grandfather, Henry Jung. With the advance money in his pocket, he would purchase gravestones for each of them. They had been buried by their own kind as outcasts for associating with whites. Even then, none of their Chinese relatives would have anything to do with either Jack or his sister: "They put us on the 'outcast' list the day we were born."

On the morning of June 5, 1981, Jack Henry Abbott, wearing a winter suit of pinstripes his sister had purchased for him, walked away from eighteen years of adult prison and five years of juvenile detention. Frances Amador was nearly in tears as she greeted her brother. Jack looked so pale and emaciated. "Some things," she thought, "had gone out of him" after so many years in prison and in solitary. "They were bound to."[10] He was thirty-six years old, the same age as Gary Gilmore at the time of his release in the spring of 1976. All Jack wanted to do, he vowed, was to lose himself in literature.

13

No Paradiso

"Didn't you learn anything from writing about Gary Gilmore?" Norris Church, Norman's wife, asked him. "Somebody who has been in prison his whole life can't just change and be a normal person overnight."[1] Although Norris was undoubtedly aware of her husband's nearly three-year correspondence with a prisoner, she had no idea that Mailer had agreed to give Abbott a job upon his release and have him move to New York City. She worried about the details as Norman prepared to drive out to JFK to meet Jack's plane and bring him to dinner at their Brooklyn home. Unfortunately, Jack was not placed in one of the better halfway houses in the city, where he might have gradually adapted to "civilian" life. First slated for one on the Upper West Side, he was rejected because of his violent record. Instead, he was released from solitary to the city in one of its worst, crime-ridden neighborhoods. Ironically, almost to the day of Jack's stabbing of Richard Adan in that neighborhood, *The New York Times* ran a piece lauding the halfway house in the posh upper Broadway neighborhoods as one of the most successful "in the city that try to smooth the transition from prison to life outside."[2]

Jack had been assigned to the Salvation Army halfway house at 1 East Third Street, then in the worst section of Manhattan. Located in the Bowery, it was one of the highest-crime precincts in the city. He described the neighborhood as a "human zoo." One night that summer, while he was talking to somebody in front of the halfway house, a car across the street was firebombed. On other occasions, while patronizing a delicatessen on the corner of Second Avenue and Fourth Street, he witnessed at least three stabbings. "The ambulance was always howling through the neighborhood." Derelicts and addicts slept on the sidewalks. Some residents in the halfway house, aware of his newly earned notoriety as an author, would volunteer to run errands for him. He couldn't walk ten feet, he said, without being hassled. "Crazy bastards preaching the Bible, screaming *in my face*." Often when out on the streets, someone would shout, "There goes Jack!" He went into a rage when his new black shoes were stolen from his room at the halfway house. He finally decided to arm himself with a knife for self-protection. According to Robert Sam Anson, who wrote about the Abbott case in *Life* magazine after the stabbing of Adan and Jack's recapture, Abbott was drinking and doing drugs down in the Bowery. "His favorite hangouts were Phebe's, a popular actors' spot, and the Great Jones, a gathering place for dancers, among them a young man named Richard Adan." Jack generally came alone to the Great Jones, had dinner and more than a few drinks. The waitresses took him to be a merchant seaman. He also frequented a nearby discotheque inhabited by prostitutes and transsexuals. Still a "situational homosexual" because of prison life, like Gilmore who had difficulty engaging in normal heterosexual intercourse after his release, Jack was seen at least once with what police described as a "Puerto Rican he/she."[3] To Mailer, he had spoken of at least one homosexual encounter in prison, while nevertheless assuring him that his sexual preference under "normal" conditions was heterosexual.

This crime-ridden area was his limbo until the end of August, when his federal parole was officially scheduled to begin. The halfway house had fairly strict rules, but they were easily broken—allowing inmates to go back out on the streets after curfew as long as they were present in the morning for roll call. Norris remembered the first time he came for dinner, dressed in his winter suit in the summertime—in fact, one similar to the kind Mailer himself wore. "Hi, I'm Jack," he said, as he entered the apartment, looking somewhat gaunt and tense. Norris remembered him as tall, "slim, neat, and nervous." She couldn't tell what ethnicity he was, but she thought "he had a slightly exotic look, with tan skin, and was much more attractive than [she] had anticipated . . . He ate every scrap on his plate and had seconds," telling his hostess it was the best meal he ever had.[4]

He came back to their Brooklyn home for dinner several times and once got permission to take the bus up to the Mailers' summer home in Provincetown on Cape Cod. At one Brooklyn meal, actually a dinner party with several distinguished guests, the recent ex-convict met Patricia Lawford, sister of the late President Kennedy. Other guests that evening were Jean Malaquais, Mailer's

Marxist mentor of an earlier day, his fifteen-year-old daughter, and the writer Dotson Rader, known for his anti-Vietnam stance in writings Jack admired. (Abbott abhorred what he called America's murder of a "doll-like people.") Pat Lawford became annoyed when Jack started badmouthing the United States as "a fascist hell-hole." When he said he intended to emigrate to Cuba, Lawford offered to buy him a one-way ticket. "That night," Norris recalled, "was the first real inkling we had of what we were up against." Indeed, she already thought they "had a big problem on their hands."[5] Jack became fond of Norris, as well as of her three-year-old son, John Buffalo, who as an adult today still recalls the attention he received from this strange man. Jack also pestered Norris with petty requests regarding the simplest everyday tasks.

Moreover, as it turned out, Jack and Norman were better epistolary friends than they were in the flesh. Mailer had already returned to writing his Egyptian book, what he thought would be his magnum opus, but he also didn't enjoy Jack's company that much and felt like a babysitter instead of the literary mentor he had become in the last three years. Jack was not as interesting in person as he was on paper, a fact he had modestly warned Mailer about early in their correspondence. "What struck me most," Mailer later commented, "is that in contrast to his [writing] style, which is often so clear, he could never finish a sentence or be definite about anything when he spoke."[6] During his visit to the Mailers in Provincetown, Abbott sat out on their deck overlooking the bay for hours at a time, as if he had never in his life seen the ocean before. (In fact, he had never seen the Atlantic but vaguely claimed to Mailer in one of his letters that he had been to Los Angeles and seen the Pacific Ocean.)

Although some of the staff at Random House, where Jack occasionally visited Erroll McDonald, were initially unnerved at having a convicted felon in their midst, it apparently never occurred to any of the Mailer family members—for example, to the author's two daughters from his second marriage, who took Jack to the movies in Provincetown one evening—that they should be afraid. Danielle Mailer, then twenty-four, remembered that Jack was "socially unskilled, but very respectful." At the same time, he exhibited the anxiety of a "caged animal." During the movie, he got up four or five times, returning, "sniffing and snorting like he had taken cocaine."[7] As he became more comfortable with the Mailer extended family on the Cape, far from both prison life and even the halfway house he already hated, he talked about his life in prison, even about the time he had killed somebody with a knife who had "disrespected" him. It was strange behavior for someone who planned to change his name and never admit he'd been in prison. Norris nervously dismissed such talk as the bragging of "a little boy." In fairness to Abbott, it should be noted that Norris Church's remembrances of Jack do not altogether square with what he told Mailer after returning to prison—in response, for example, to one press report that he had "regaled" her with prison stories.

Abbott was something of a phenomenon in New York City—an ex-con raised behind bars about to publish a bestselling book, already hyped as such in the press. He followed the actor Dudley Moore on *Good Morning America* with Mailer; was photographed by Jill Krementz, known for her pictures of famous authors; and interviewed by *People*, *Rolling Stone*, and the *Soho Weekly News*. He visited the city's museums, including the Metropolitan Museum of Art and the Frick Collection. Abbott's story, it was suggested, even deserved a movie—perhaps with Robert De Niro or Christopher Walken in the lead. Here was the latest Camus, Genet, or Solzhenitsyn—the great writer finally emancipated. *In the Belly of the Beast* was slated for official publication on July 18, but in spite of all the attention he was receiving, everyone concerned with Jack urged him to go slow. Only two months before, he had been confined to solitary at Draper; now, he was free in the Big Apple. As he later told Mailer, "I came from max. security—after *3 years* of solitary—straight away into that artificial monster called Manhattan."[8] He had brought along his hair-trigger temper to New York City, where strangers weren't always the most polite people, not on the street at least. The noise of Manhattan alone must have been toxic to him after the relative silence of solitary. "It's a long time since a convict has come out of jail with as many years as you have, and writes as well as you do," Mailer, perhaps somewhat anxiously, had told him on April 27, 1981. Jack suffered from "sensory deprivation" after so many years in prison. He advised him to beware of what they both regarded as prison paranoia. Mailer also advised Jack to stay off any more TV shows, as he was hardly ready for the everyday tasks of a free person. When Norris took him shopping, he asked her whether there would be someone present to "issue" clothes to him. As awkward as the newly released Gilmore had been in his plastic prison shoes, Jack was somewhat incredulous that he could try on trousers with no one "watching."[9]

"He was a man in a different universe," editor Erroll McDonald remembered.[10] When they first met in June of 1981 and had coffee near Central Park, Abbott was scandalized by female joggers in what he considered "sluttish" dress. When the two repaired to Macy's for Jack to purchase trousers, he wasn't so friendly to the clerk. Angered that the alterations to his purchase couldn't be done immediately, Abbott asked for a pair of scissors so he could do it himself on the spot. Abbott, McDonald said, was "a man on edge." During one of their meetings, he noticed that Abbott wore a knife strapped to his leg. He seemed to live in his own world. He had the capacity to function or focus amid the kind of distractions that would deter normal people. This behavior, or ability, doubtless stemmed from his long years in noisy prisons, where he had developed such powers of concentration.

Gary Fisketjon, a colleague of McDonald's at Random House, also remembered Abbott as a stranger in the free world—"a fish out of a fishbowl."[11] At one point while in Macy's, Erroll had told him, the newly released prisoner saw collapsible umbrellas for sale and wondered why the store was selling "clubs." That summer, Fisketjon had several literary (and personal) conversations with Abbott, who attended at least one of the parties he threw at his East Village apartment, which was only a few blocks away from the halfway house. Abbott usually came to them with McDonald.

When in a crowded room during such a party, Fisketjon recalled, Abbott was careful to never show his back to other people, standing instead in a corner near the door. He never talked to anybody he didn't know. On the New York streets, he was shocked by the kind of rude behavior one might normally encounter there. You didn't dare talk or act like that on the "inside," Abbott frequently observed, because in prison such rudeness was inevitably followed by physical violence.

Not long after his visit to Provincetown, on July 9, Random House arranged a literary dinner—a rather routine ritual for noted authors in those days—to celebrate the imminent publication of *In the Belly of the Beast*. It was held at Il Mulino in Greenwich Village. Mailer and his wife attended, along with Erroll McDonald; Jason Epstein, the editor in chief of Random House; and Robert Silvers, whose *New York Review of Books* had already published two essays by Jack as well as what would become Mailer's introduction to *In the Belly of the Beast*. The celebratory dinner was low-key, according to McDonald, who said they drank white wine, not champagne. Silvers described Abbott on the occasion as "very shy and withdrawn—extremely silent."[12] One other who attended the celebratory dinner for Abbott, no doubt with a certain hesitation, was Jerzy Kosinski. Their meeting had to be awkward in view of Abbott's earlier verbal assault on Kosinski, which had naturally concluded their prison correspondence. Kosinski, a survivor of postwar communism in Poland, rejected Jack's beloved Stalinism. In fact, Abbott had told Mailer on October 15, 1978, that the last letter he had written Kosinski was "even couched in threats on his life." Kosinski had further angered Abbott by sending him a copy of his latest novel, which had profited from their correspondence. Yet Abbott hastened to assure Mailer that "by no stretch of the imagination could I be angry at your use of my letters [in *The Executioner's Song*]."

During his brief time in New York City and out of prison, Jack befriended two young women. Veronique de St. Andre was from France; Susan Roxas was from the Philippines and a student at Barnard College. Back in prison after the trial for killing Richard Adan, Abbott spoke wistfully of them to Mailer. Susan Roxas, whose father owned a large investment firm in the Philippines, lived in the East Village near Malaquais, who had become a mentor to Jack upon his release, and indeed beforehand through correspondence. Jack found both women beautiful and charming, relieved finally to be in the company of women instead of men, and "not have to put up with the phony tough-guy shit."[13]

He was doing fine, he said, once he'd met these two attractive young women. "I started shunning everyone after I met Veronique—she had a place right *next door* to the ½ house. Then I met Susan Roxas and that is when I stopped spending any time at the ½ house."[14] The two women, he thought, knew everything about art and literature. "Veronique," he told Mailer in May of 1982, "used to read me poetry in French and played Mozart for me at her place and Susan is all brains—literature graduate from Barnard who looks like a Siamese princess—god, she is beautiful."

He never introduced them to anyone at the halfway house—"because Veronique was afraid of them and didn't want to be friendly with them." He got himself a puppy, which he called "Precious," and he would walk the pet over to Washington Square. Sometimes Veronique would accompany him. He was writing, he claimed, in his room in the halfway house and visiting the galleries in Soho, "usually with someone I'd meet in the park." He was given a free pass to the Westside YMCA, where he exercised a few times. And once or twice he had lunch with Silvers. Abbott, it appears, was afloat with his freedom after so many years.

It was Friday evening of July 17, 1981, that Jack went dancing at a German beer garden with the two women. During the evening, Roxas noticed the knife Jack carried to protect himself at the halfway house. Early the next morning, they ended up at the Binibon, a cramped all-night restaurant about three blocks from the halfway house, on the corner of Second Avenue and Fifth Street. The place wasn't especially known for its good service or manners, though that reputation may have been due to the behavior of its late-night clientele. The slightly built twenty-two-year-old Cuban-born Richard Adan was its night manager and son-in-law of the owner, Henry Howard. His parents were Cuban émigrés. The previous February, Adan had married Howard's stepdaughter, Ricci, an actress and choreographer. Just back from Spain, where he had participated in a series for public television, he had also recently finished a play about the Lower East Side for production the following season at La Mama experimental theater. Nearing the end of his "graveyard shift" that morning, he called his wife to say that he was finishing up and would be home soon, adding that his last customers were "three people—a guy and two girls."[15] Adan either waited on the party himself or came over to the table to assist the waiter. While the two women were focused on their menus, they noticed that Abbott and Adan appeared to be having some kind of disagreement. Though he later denied it, Jack had asked to use the bathroom, which was reserved for employees only. When he protested, raising his voice, Adan asked him to step outside—not to fight, as Abbott later testified, but for a chance to calm down and be directed to an alley where he might relieve himself behind a Dumpster. William Majeski, the detective who had just come off duty at the Ninth Precinct station in the Lower East Side early that morning, speculates that Abbott was embarrassed at being refused use of the facilities in front of his female companions, and as a result addressed his emerging anger at Adan, who was apparently talking to Jack in a subdued voice, hoping not to alarm any customers or passersby as the two exited the restaurant. Majeski, who considered Abbott a "mean man" who was disliked by his former cellmates, thinks that this embarrassment led to the attack on the unarmed Adan.[16]

At his trial for second-degree murder, Abbott claimed that Adan also carried a knife, or appeared to have one, which he said evidently got swept away by street cleaners before it could be recovered. In *My Return*, in which Abbott agonizingly recounts the details of their clash on the pavement outside the restaurant, Adan clearly has a knife. An eyewitness to the killing, however, observed only Abbott's weapon. The time was about 5:00 A.M. on the morning of July 18. Wayne Larson, an itinerant Vietnam veteran who was staying at his sister's place and supporting himself with odd jobs, testified that Abbott stabbed Adan after a brief exchange of angry words. Adan, perceiving that he had gotten much more than he bargained for by engaging Abbott, apparently started to walk away from the ex-con and toward the restaurant. As he did, Abbott "made a beeline" for Adan and attacked him from the rear. Grabbing his neck, Abbott reached around and stabbed Adan in the chest "with terrific velocity." Abbott moved with the quickness of a boxer, his hand speed remarkable. His attack on Adan was so quick and powerful that he may have sliced Adan's heart in two. While Abbott, perhaps not yet aware that the stabbing had been fatal, taunted the wounded figure, Adan—according to the witness—muttered "God, no. Are you crazy?" and "You didn't have to kill me," before slumping to the pavement. Then Abbott ran back into the restaurant and shouted to his two female companions, "I just killed a man," and urged them to run with him.[17]

Everything went up in smoke. Later, after he had been returned to prison as a result of a first-degree manslaughter conviction, an interviewer suggested to him that on July 18, he had had everything going for him. Free after nineteen years in prison, he had just published a book that *The New York Times* would call "brilliant." Mailer, one of America's most famous authors, was acting as his sponsor. "Dante writes about the *Vita Nuova*," Peter Manso told Abbott, who went through two packs of cigarettes during their three-hour interview through a prison screen in the noisy prison visiting room, "the new life—a form of deliverance. You had everything laid out in front of you. Why did you fuck it up?" Abbott answered: "Because I didn't get delivered to no paradiso—they didn't put me in the right place. They delivered me right back to prison."[18] In one sense, the authorities *had* set up Abbott for failure by placing him in a crime-ridden part of the city, yet his actual reoffending—the stabbing of Adan—probably had little or nothing to do with the neighborhood, except that the neighborhood perhaps stirred up his sense of prison paranoia.

14

In the Belly of the Beast: An Analysis and Autopsy

In the acknowledgments to *In the Belly of the Beast:* *Letters from Prison*, Jack thanked his sister, who "saw me through everything described in this book, and has kept something alive in me that would otherwise have perished long ago." The statement is true in the sense that Frances Amador stuck by her brother to his dying day, helping him even in death by casting doubt on the prison spokesman's assertion at the Wende Correctional Facility in New York that Abbott took his own life. Over the many years of his incarceration, she had visited him but irregularly because of the great distances often between her and the state or federal prison her brother happened to be in. Abbott chronicled his emotional and intellectual development in prison over the years through letters to Frances, who died in 2016. She was the first person he saw when he got out of Draper in 1981. She had been his only lifeline—for twenty-five years or more—until he found Mailer, who is not thanked in the acknowledgments. The only other person Abbott recognizes here is his editor at Random

House, Erroll McDonald. Mailer, who wrote the introduction, is, of course, mentioned in what is essentially a reconstruction of many of the letters originally sent to him between 1978 and 1980.

The book is dedicated to a number of legendary prisoners, including George Jackson and Gary Gilmore—"that they may rest in peace." One other equally notorious prisoner named—for political acts of violence during the Vietnam War—is Sam Melville. Born Samuel Joseph Grossman, he took up Herman Melville's surname as well as the seething anger of two of the writer's most memorable protagonists: Bartleby of Wall Street and Ahab of the whaling industry out of Nantucket. Convicted of bombing various buildings in New York City, Melville had perished in the Attica riots of 1971.

Before beginning his story, Jack provides his own introduction, or "foreword," by quoting Friedrich Engels from *Anti-Dühring* (1877), where, acting as Karl Marx's spokesman, he condemns the Utopian socialist Eugen Dühring for advocating peaceful social change over that wrought by revolution. Engels used the fable of Adam in the Garden of Eden with a second Adam instead of an Eve, thereby forming a relationship that cannot bear fruit—"that to Herr Dühring will be left the uncontested glory of having constructed his original sin with two men."[1] In other words, Abbott is hinting that nothing short of violence will repair the social fabric in America that raised him as a "state-raised convict." This allusion to Engels and Dühring, as it turned out, served as a scary omen, for Jack's first major act as a revolutionary on the outside was to kill Richard Adan for "disrespecting" him. Without this fateful incident, Abbott would have possibly emigrated to Cuba, then about to be placed on the U.S. list of state sponsors for terrorism for assisting leftist insurgencies in the southern hemisphere. In fact, he was trying to get there when he fled to Mexico in the late summer of 1981.

The first chapter is entitled "State-Raised Convict," a phrase denoting a legacy and the argument Abbott would use in his defense in the trial for killing Adan. The phrase implies not only the dehumanizing process of prison but also the domestic and financial impoverishment that are its necessary preparations—the broken home and the often heartless foster homes, the juvenile centers and reform schools. As Sue M. Halpern wrote in her July 4 review in *The Nation*, the first judge to sentence the preadolescent Abbott to his first detention became a "hanging judge," who ensured the kind of socialization that keeps our prisons brimming to capacity and beyond. Halpern reviewed *In the Belly* along with Ed Bunker's *Little Boy Blue* (1981), a semifictional account of a child raised in the same gruesome circumstances as Abbott. Both tales present American prisons as gulags, "but it is Jack Abbott's story that emerges as larger than life and must not be treated as fiction."

In the Belly of the Beast is composed as letters with "you" as the addressee throughout. It's the colloquial, of course, but in this case the colloquy was first with Norman Mailer. "I've wanted somehow," Abbott began, "to convey to you the sensations—the atmospheric pressure, you might say—of what it is to be seriously a long-term prisoner in an American prison."[2] Abbott has been in prison for so long, he says, that he can barely remember what he did wrong in the first place—except perhaps to have been born of the wrong parents. Anyway, it's been so long that freedom is almost as unimaginable as life after death, or "heaven," might be—he has been free only in his dreams. Ironically, during his one taste of freedom at the time of his 1971 escape from Draper, he dreamed of nothing but prison while sleeping on the outside.

Abbott claims he didn't come to talk about "these feelings" until he corresponded with Mailer. They were simply too personal, too deeply embedded in his psyche. Indeed, his book became a reality only when the possibility of release also came about. "I am at this moment thirty-seven years old . . . I would estimate that I have served a good fourteen or fifteen years in solitary."[3] Yet the life of imprisonment started earlier for this "state-raised convict." His first formal "crime" was the failure to adjust to foster care—as he had run away from home after home. Talking about prison, he stresses, is painful because his imprisonment began when he was a child in reform school: "I served five years in the big red-brick building, and altogether [for repeatedly attempting to escape] two or three in solitary confinement. When I walked out, I was considered an adult, subject to adult laws."[4]

Presenting himself first as a child in prison creates a forceful argument against the incarceration of minors and, by extension, prison itself. Many prisoners with long terms such as Abbott's, it is implied, began either as innocent children or redeemable adults. Abbott recalls his first unsuccessful escape from the Utah State Industrial School. Caught and strip-searched, pinned helplessly naked to the floor, the assaulting guard "inspects my anus and my private parts, and I watch, anxiously, hoping with all my might he does not hurt me there." This boy prisoner never really grows up or matures, but is always angry, always resistant to authority. Abbott the writer takes this anger right into his book and will never get beyond it to live a normal life. "Transcend or die," Barry Scheck, of the Innocence Project, advises those whom DNA tests have liberated.[5] Jack believed himself to be entirely innocent and thus wrongly convicted, like so many of the men later freed through DNA.

It is this boy-man ratio that dramatizes and energizes what could otherwise simply have been another litany of complaints by an ex-prisoner. Abbott insists that during his entire twenty-five years in prison, he has never been able to adjust. "I have never gone a month in prison without incurring disciplinary action for violating 'rules.' Not in all these years."[6] It was simply the response by a man "who does not belong" in prison. What saved him were books. Through them, Abbott assuaged, or better yet, accommodated his anger. Reading Karl Marx taught him about the evils and injustices of a capitalistic society whose prisons were "prison-industrial complexes." Taught in prison that Marx lied, inmates were given "education programs" to teach them what the authorities want them to learn. "I pride myself," Abbott writes and places the sentence in italics, "on the fact that I've never been in a prison school."[7] He also insists both in and out of his book that he never broke the law as an adult, which was not true either before or after his release in 1981.

Like Sam Melville, Jack Henry Abbott took on the identity of one of Melville's resisters to accentuate his anger at society. Like

Herman Melville's doomed resister in "Bartleby the Scrivener," Abbott "prefers not to." The 1853 short story, surprisingly modern in its spiritual relativism, concerns a male secretary who (before the invention of the typewriter and the entrance of women as "typewriters" in the offices of America) takes a job as a copyist in a law office on Wall Street. His desk faces "a small side-window" which opens to a brick wall. In other words, his life is "walled in"—limited symbolically to the normal, ultimately meaningless choices of life. He refuses to work, which in this case means copying as a scrivener endless and (to him) meaningless law briefs and documents dealing with "rich men's bonds and mortgages and title deeds." (Following the disappointing critical and financial failure of *Moby-Dick* in 1851, Melville himself would eventually become walled in to a lowly job in the New York City customhouse, walking the docks.) Although Bartleby's employer is compassionate, he cannot save his disillusioned employee. Bartleby is arrested for vagrancy after he refuses to vacate the law offices that his employer has already vacated in order to cut his ties with Bartleby as an employee. He is confined to the Tombs prison on Broadway, where executions were still carried out. After his death by starvation (preferring not to eat either), the reader learns that Bartleby's last job had been in the Dead Letter Office in Washington, D.C. "Dead letters! Does it not sound like dead men?" Melville asks. Bartleby has run out of psychic gas. He has lost the will to live because he refuses to obey random authority; he resists. Abbott resists in prison because his choices are all bad ones, whereas for Melville's Bartleby, life itself is a prison where all the choices are also equally bad ones.

In the chapter "The Varieties of Punishment," Abbott insists that nobody has the right to take away his soul, his identity. That's what prison tries to do—make the prisoner a stranger to his desires and needs. Depersonalization arises from deprivation. Abbott expresses nostalgia for a time when he envisions that prisoners tried to help each other, because they were still people with identifiable personalities. If endless routine and predictable cruelty from guards don't undercut the person of the inmate, behavioral drugs do. Regular doses of Mellaril prevent the production of sperm. "If you masturbate," he writes, and somehow achieve "a fantasy erection," you experience at orgasm every sensation "you should experience, but with this difference: absolutely no substance issues . . . no fluid at all, let alone semen."[8] And there comes a time when you become nearly inured to physical punishment.

Talking of his years in solitary, he says that nobody so confined ever *faces* another prisoner, but you always hear them. "I have 'seen' *wars* take place in the hole. I have seen sexual love take place in the hole." Otherwise, you sit not only in your own nothingness but that of the society that sent you there. "Time descends in your cell like the lid of a coffin." The same treatment for animals in a zoo, he contends, would bring charges of cruelty to animals from the Humane Society. Once released to the general population, there is no intimacy to make up for the sensory deprivation resulting from the hole. For the prisoner who does not engage in situational homosexuality, bodily contact is prison combat."[9]

Only at night, after "lights out," is there relative peace in prison, not only from the constant threats of violence from both guards and inmates but also the noise that seems to vibrate your brain. The downside, however, is that you can't read. The only diversions are hearing "the pigs making their rounds . . . [their] keychains, the dogs they bring on the count. You hear the sleeping sounds of the prisoners." Some convicts, he states, finally agree to anything to protect themselves—"You'll suck every cock in the cell house to 'get along.' " Once you cross that line and submit, there is no returning. Those who do wince whenever a guard or another prisoner passes them. Broken men, they fill their days filling the needs of their masters. Most convicts, he writes, don't cross that line. Instead, you keep yourself ready to kill to maintain your manhood. The knife is the most "intimate and useful weapon for self-protection."[10] Here, Abbott goes into describing the routine of targeting his victim (material which will be used against him in the Adan trial).

The weakest part of *In the Belly of the Beast* is the second half, where Abbott reveals his naïve interests in communism and his admiration for Mao and Stalin. This material most likely did not come from his letters to Mailer, aside from their occasional rants on the subject. No doubt, when some of the letters that were lost by Mailer's secretary were reconstructed for *In the Belly of the Beast*, Abbott was allowed to fill out the book, which isn't that long, with his denunciation of the United States and corresponding praise of repressive communist countries such as Red China and the Soviet Union. Running through the entire book is Abbott's rage for his treatment in the United States since a boy, which ignores the fact that he was a resister at every turn in his development from foster homes through reform school to the penitentiary. Most victims of domestic circumstances like Abbott's don't become convicts. Many overcome the harshness of their early environments and find a path to relative success or satisfaction in life. But more than a few do follow Abbott, though perhaps not as far. Gilmore, for example, was a product of his rough upbringing. Both became killers, and both were artists who attracted the eye of Norman Mailer. Although Mailer never met Gilmore, he did come to know him through Abbott, who, as a result of the correspondence between Mailer and Abbott, constitutes a silent presence in *The Executioner's Song*.

In spite of its hardy sales, reviews of *In the Belly of the Beast* are relatively sparse, perhaps because of the Adan stabbing, which occurred at the same time the book was released in the summer of 1981. More than a few venues may have canceled their reviews after it became known that Jack had killed a waiter and was on the lam. The best one—in *The New York Times* and discussed in chapter 15—came out only a day after the Adan killing and was overwhelmingly favorable.

Significantly, Jack Beatty's review in *The New Republic* of August 4 added a last-minute postscript about Abbott's being sought for questioning in the death of Richard Adan. Otherwise, the review was a mixture of faint praise and robust condemnation, calling *In the Belly of the Beast* both "disturbing" and full of "baby talk Marxist jabber." Abbott was as "besotted by theory," Beatty thought, as Jerzy Kosinski's Chauncey Gardiner of *Being There* (1971) was by television. The review, however, did note with some alarm Abbott's bitter tone—his "fierce, angry voice, full of hatred and defiance," fuming up from "a depth of indignity that few of us could imagine." The real target of the reviewer's attack was Mailer himself, who, with Abbott, was simply saluting, as he had in "The White Negro," the existential daring of the criminal—"Existential daring—this from a man who probably hasn't ridden a subway in 30 years and whose idea of violence is a catty confrontation with Gore Vidal." He also criticized Robert Silvers of *The New York Review of Books* for endorsing a book that was, despite its display of writing talent, partly unreadable because of its Marxist rants. J. D. Reed, in *Time* magazine (July 20, 1981), thought Abbott's admiration for Marx and Engels ingenuous, but conceded that his prison letters "belong with the best prison literature, not because of their accounts of atrocity, but for their disturbing picture of daily life behind bars." It was this aspect of Abbott's letters that most influenced Mailer in writing *The Executioner's Song*: even when Gilmore is released from prison, he is never free of its demons.

Once Abbott had fled and been captured, the reviews became more negative than positive. The newspaper coverage of the trial also hurt him, deadening any sympathy readers of his book might have been disposed to have. Worse yet, during his trial, Abbott took the stand in his own defense and further blighted his case. "Not a cough sounded [in the courtroom] as Abbott, 37, gave some grisly details of the aftermath of the 5 a.m. stabbing outside the Binibon restaurant where Adan had worked," wrote *Time* magazine

(January 25, 1982). As Abbott tried to explain away the killing as a "tragic misunderstanding," Adan's father-in-law, Henry Howard, rose in the courtroom and shouted, "You intended it, you scum! You scum, you useless piece of shit. You and Mailer and all the [other] creeps." Mailer, who testified at the trial, maintained his support of his doomed protégé, and his literary reputation, never separate from his personal history, took yet another beating.

Writing in the London *New Statesman* of February 5, 1982, Michael Mewshaw took a dim view of Abbott and his book. American reviews, this American expatriate wrote, ignored such "non-textual" information as Abbott's long criminal record in prison. "Like most American prisoners," Mewshaw continued, "he would probably have been paroled early, but he was prone to violence, repeatedly tried to escape, and provoked the guards by his throwing food, urine, and feces. Then he murdered a fellow convict and wounded another." Felice Picano, in a 1,500-word review entitled "The Prison of the Mind" in the *New York Native*, a biweekly gay newspaper, of September 21, 1981, saw the record quite differently, saying that the "facts behind Jack's Abbott's book are bleakly simple. Placed in a juvenile detention home at age eleven because he could not adjust to the absurdities of the foster home system, Abbott became a criminal."

Picano had few problems with Jack's complaints about prison. What he took issue with was Abbott's attitude toward homosexuality, or situational homosexuality in Abbott's case. While he agreed with Mewshaw's point about Jack's becoming his worst enemy by "preferring not to," he also censured Abbott on his hypocritical and condescending view of homosexuals as—in prison, at least—"women." He was dismayed to hear Abbott declare that homosexuality in prison was "almost always connected with aggression and humiliation." The reviewer saw Abbott as simply naive about (his own) homosexuality and defensive of his role as a tough con who abuses weaker inmates. In fact, Picano wrote, "nothing of what he writes squares with what I've heard from men who have been imprisoned, nor does it tally with the best studies of homosexuality I've read." Like many reviewers, on many other subjects in the book aside from the slow death of prison that Abbott so superbly describes, Picano doubted Abbott on the facts, or, at best, thought he was exaggerating if not also distorting minor details that didn't support his overall story.

Probably the soberest review was an academic one appearing in the *Michigan Law Review* of March 1983. Viewed as an artifact of institutionalization, *In the Belly of the Beast* "demonstrates—if only by a single example—a bitter but essential lesson for penal policy makers: Do not confine whom you would not destroy." Writing in hindsight of the verdict and sentence, the review touched on the central nervous system of the entire Abbott debacle. Years of prison, it suggested, had rendered Jack Henry Abbott incapable of nonviolent freedom. Regardless of his remarkable talent as an autodidact and writer, he had become damaged goods long before not only his 1981 release but also his interchange with Mailer that led up to it. (There are many indications in the actual letters to Mailer that Jack was still dangerous—signs that Mailer evidently chose to ignore in the light of Abbott's literary talent.) Abbott became a ruined man possibly as early as 1967, when he killed James Christensen, perhaps indeed even as early as his graduation from reform school, when, as he wrote in his book, he was considered "reformed" and "subject to adult laws."[11]

15

Running

The day after Jack Abbott stabbed Richard Adan and effectively sealed his fate as a prison lifer, the Sunday *New York Times* of July 19 published its enthusiastic review of *In the Belly of the Beast: Letters from Prison*. Jack didn't become aware of it for many weeks. He was surprised as much by the sympathy his tale had aroused as by the initial sales. His horrifying description of American prisons in the twentieth century had called forth from the reviewer a condemnation that could have served for the German death camps Terrence Des Pres had written about so vividly. Even after more than a quarter of a century, *In the Belly of the Beast* strikes a sharp blow at prison conditions in America.

Des Pres, then the William Henry Crawshaw Professor of Literature at Colgate University, deemed Abbott's condemnation of America's "Maximum Security inferno" "awesome, brilliant, perversely ingenious." Lauding it as "an articulation of penal nightmare," he declared it "completely compelling." The author of *The Survivor: An Anatomy of the Death Camps*, Des Pres described Abbott as "a child of the state." His first crime, Des Pres noted, was being born as the offspring of a prostitute. "The next was 'failure to adjust' to the string of foster homes that passed him along; at age nine, therefore, he was sent to juvenile detention centers, and at twelve made the leap to reform schools. At age eighteen he was abruptly set loose, all the world before him. Six months later he entered his first penitentiary . . . Between the ages of twelve and thirty-seven he lived free for a total of nine and a half months." Des Pres essentially rehearsed what would become Jack's defense in his trial for stabbing Adan. "By his own definition, Jack Abbott is a 'state-raised convict,'" somebody "reared by the state" to learn over and over again "that people in society can do anything to him and not be punished by the law."[1]

At the end of his review, however, Des Pres wondered whether Abbott could survive his newfound freedom, whether he could ever write so well again about anything other than prison. Could he write without the anger and rage that had propelled *In the Belly of the Beast*? By the time Des Pres's review was in the hands of most of its readers, Jack was already in Philadelphia, on the run toward Texas and Mexico with the hope of emigrating from Mexico City to Cuba. For word of his assault upon Adan was soon to get out. The next day, *The New York Times* followed up its glowing review of Abbott's book with this headline: "Convict-Author Known by Mailer Is Being Sought in Fatal Stabbing."

After killing Adan, Abbott raced back to his room at the Salvation Army halfway house a few blocks from the Binibon to grab two hundred dollars he had hidden there. He took a cab to the Port Authority terminal, intending to take a bus out of the city.

Once there, however, he decided he needed all his money and took another cab to a Citibank branch at Lexington and Fifty-fourth Street, forgetting that it was Saturday and banks were closed. (This was the era before ATMs.) There, he had deposited a thousand dollars, funds from his publishing advance.

Before fleeing New York City, Abbott kept a Sunday brunch date at the Upper East Side apartment of Jean Malaquais and his wife, perhaps stalling while he figured out his next step in escaping the city. He had even called Mailer in Provincetown, but the author said he was half asleep (at 6:00 A.M. Saturday morning) and asked Abbott to call him back. Jack said nothing to Jean and his wife about the fatal encounter with Adan. Rather, Malaquais later told the police, he calmly talked about literature and related matters. Yet Jack did inquire about the best way to get out of the city, and Malaquais mentioned that buses ran from Staten Island to New Jersey. Upon leaving Malaquais's apartment, he took a ferry to Staten Island and caught the bus to New Jersey, only to learn once aboard that it first took him back to the Port Authority terminal. As a result, he caught the very next bus leaving the terminal, this one to Philadelphia, where he continued his escape to the Southwest and Mexico. Abbott was again free but on the lam, just as he had been during those six weeks as a fugitive from Draper. "Running," he told authorities after his final capture in September, "is the only thing I've known about the outside."[2]

His father's relatives lived in the Texas Panhandle, but Abbott, who as a teenager had once been cruelly rejected and scorned when he visited them, considered them "pigs" and went directly to the border of Mexico. Once inside the country (around July 22), he made for Mexico City and spent a week moving through the villages of the nearby state of Puebla looking for a place to stay. By now, he had little of the two hundred dollars left. He returned to Mexico City and its then-trendy Zona Rosa district. There, he met an American named Griffin, who was essentially begging on the streets, playing a guitar for whatever change pedestrians might drop in his guitar case. Jack figured that this guy must know his way around the city, for a "gringo beggar" in Mexico, as he told Mailer, was risking imprisonment. Hoping that Griffin could help get him passage to Cuba with the British passport of Griffin's friend, he bought him a drink and later accompanied him to his rented room in a run-down part of the city near the presidential palace. Griffin, an alcoholic who apparently came from a wealthy family, was ultimately unable to help Abbott, and they eventually parted in Vera Cruz. This meeting occurred in late July, about a week after the stabbing. While together, Griffin discovered Abbott was a fugitive when he read about him in an outdated issue of *The New York Times.* Whether this information led to their parting is not known, but Jack was armed with a revolver.

Abbott made his way back to the Texas border and then over to New Orleans, where he worked as a hot dog vendor in the French Quarter under the name of Jack Eastman. He befriended a Greek prostitute named Ruby while frequenting the Greek bars in a red-light district. Back in prison, Jack may have suspected that Ruby had been the one to notify the authorities about his whereabouts after he eventually left the city, but she did not know where he had fled. According to Detective William J. Majeski, who interviewed her, she simply felt sorry for him because he didn't have any money. She was supposed to use her connections with the Greek sea captains to smuggle Jack out of the country, and even though she pitied him, she was probably happy to try to get rid of him. Also, by this time Jack's resolve to remain free may have weakened. His only hope, it seemed, was a ship out of New Orleans, which would take him to Cuba. Another prostitute testified after his capture that, while on the run, he seemed sad and lonely, at one point paying a prostitute simply to hug him.

While Abbott was still in New Orleans, Majeski got a fix on him by interviewing a network of the fugitive's acquaintances, including both former cellmates and family members, all of whom were contacted regularly during Abbott's time on the loose. "On my information obtained through a number of cultivated sources," he later stated, "I set up Abbott to be at a specific location." In fact, he tried to entice Abbott on a couple of occasions before the final capture in Morgan City. The first time occurred when Abbott was in New Orleans. Through underground sources, Majeski sent the fugitive fifty dollars (of his own money). When Abbott approached the person who was supposed to give him the cash, he became suspicious and ran away without collecting the money.

The close call led Abbott to leave New Orleans for Morgan City, Louisiana, an oil-rich port on the Gulf Coast about one hundred miles west of the Crescent City. He had hoped to get work as an unskilled laborer on one of the rigs in the Gulf of Mexico, perhaps to earn enough money to get to pay his way to Cuba. He was apprehended just outside the city at an oil-pipeline inspection yard on September 23, 1981. At the time he was working for four dollars an hour unloading pipes from a truck.

Acting on a tip from Majeski, Morgan City detectives and officers swept one of the industrial camps in Morgan City and arrested Abbott. Jack remembered the agent who had spotted him. Wearing the company's red-and-white overalls, he claimed to be bunking at the camp while waiting to work offshore. Shortly before noon on the twenty-third, while working alongside a biker, a "silent guy" from Georgia, and another named Bodie from Mississippi, Abbott was captured by nine police officers with sawed-off shotguns. Fearing he had a knife, they secured him with special thumb cuffs. Jack had planned to accompany Bodie, who was about forty, for work on an offshore rig. Both of his companions were also fugitives of one sort or another, and when the raid commenced it also scattered a number of Mexican illegals, who threw off their hard hats as they fled. As the marshals took Jack into custody, one of the workers shouted, after learning of the charges against Jack, "who cares if one New Yorker kills another!"[3]

Majeski had been on the case from the very beginning, having been the first detective on the scene of the Adan slaying. He had immediately sympathized with the victim. "I've seen a lot of bodies," he told Peter Manso, "but this was different. Although Adan was twenty-two, he looked younger, and his face, the expression, was angelic. Also there was a tremendous amount of blood. The knife had gone to the heart, and apparently just about every drop of blood in his body had been pumped out. There was literally a pool going from the body across the sidewalk to the curb and out into the gutter."[4]

Majeski told Mailer biographer J. Michael Lennon, "I had a lot of conversations with Richard Adan's mother early on, and with his father-in-law [Henry Howard]. I kind of found myself promising the both of them independent of each other; I promised them I would get him. Once I made that commitment, to myself, then I couldn't let go." In fact, he set up his own command post in the basement of his Staten Island home. Employing a national network of enforcement associates and acquaintances, he plotted Abbott's probable movements as he made his way to Mexico.[4] Majeski quickly read *In the Belly of the Beast* and concluded that much of what Abbott had written about prison and against guards was exaggerated. Moreover, he suspected that Abbott had plagiarized from another source on the issue of his having to eat crushed-up roaches while in solitary. He also discerned from his reading of the book the fact that Abbott "was not well-informed about life on the outside,"[5] and so began to theorize just where he might be headed. In fact, many New Yorkers concluded at the time that Abbott would flee to Mexico.

Once on the scene of the Adan slaying, Majeski, a graduate of the John Jay College of Criminal Justice and an expert in the art of interviewing suspects, identified bystanders who might know something and had uniformed police officers pull them aside for questioning. He soon questioned the two women who had been with Abbott that fateful morning who, in fact, had lingered a block away from the scene after initially fleeing the Binibon when Abbott ran. He learned Abbott's name and his address at the halfway house. Majeski also got in touch with Abbott's former cellmates at Marion, many of whom said they did not like the ex-convict. With this information, he was able to conclude that Abbott probably couldn't count on the help of any ex-cons who were now out of prison, only family and possibly people he had met following his release from Draper. In fact, Majeski soon learned that Abbott had been in touch with friends both in New York City and elsewhere, including his sister in Utah. Using the fugitive's grapevine, he sent word to him that "Majeski is looking for you."

Abbott later deeply resented Majeski's role in his capture, belittling the policeman to Mailer. In *My Return*, written with the assistance of Naomi Zack, who was married to the convict from 1990 to 1992, he challenged Majeski's statement in Manso's book that he had interviewed Abbott after his capture and return to New York. "It is our information," Abbott wrote, "that this policeman solicited film producers to buy options on the film rights to his life story as a 'crime fighter' and eventually succeeded in selling the options for an advance of five thousand dollars." (In fact, a film company did option the detective's story, but a film was never produced.)[6] In attempting to apprehend Abbott, Majeski focused on Mailer, who—the detective no doubt soon learned—had suffered his own brush with the law by stabbing his wife Adele twenty-one years earlier. Most likely, he didn't think Mailer was in any way harboring Abbott, but he did suspect that the author might have been in contact with the fugitive. He pestered Mailer through his secretary, Judith McNally, even threatening to have her boss arrested if he didn't return from Provincetown and agree to an interview. "Anytime I got a new lead or a suspicion as to where he was I would call them and say, 'Listen I've got information that Jack was seen in Chicago and I understand that he was trying to get in touch with you.'" He figured that Abbott would eventually contact Mailer, which Mailer later reluctantly told Majeski he did. "Norman," Majeski told Lennon, "was probably the least cooperative of all—maybe not least, but less than most . . ."[7]

When Abbott's trial in Manhattan began in January 1982, Mailer went on trial as well, it seemed, as far as the angry press was concerned. Here was another case of the "radical chic" that had backfired. As a result, Abbott's defense as a "state-raised convict" was somewhat drowned out. The prosecutor opened by arguing that the prison writer had essentially murdered Adan by attacking him from behind. Jack's defense lawyer and an acquaintance of Mailer's, Ivan S. Fisher, responded that the death was a "tragic accident" done in what was perceived as self-defense. Fisher read from *In the Belly of the Beast* to argue that Abbott had acted out of a prison-induced paranoia when he stabbed Adan, but the prosecution turned this approach around to convict Abbott, citing the memorable passage where he tells how to knife somebody in prison. There were also a dozen witnesses who testified to the brutality of the assault, one noting that the action was so swift that Abbott's hair flew back as he lunged at his victim. It was also noted that

Adan had been conciliatory before his stabbing, no doubt having quickly become aware that he had engaged a crazy, possibly dangerous man.

In blaming the killing on prison paranoia, Fisher argued that Jack "went from the belly of his mother to the belly of the beast." Even if the jury of seven men and five women found Abbott guilty, he said, they could decide on the basis of "extreme emotional disturbance" and reduce the second-degree murder charge to a lesser charge. Abbott had taken the stand in his own defense, and the prosecution countered that his testimony was inconsistent and full of holes, comparing parts of it with passages from *In the Belly of the Beast*. Moreover, these quoted passages also included a justification for killing in prison, because Abbott had compared prison combat to the exhilaration of sex. "That's how he gets his kicks," assistant district attorney James H. Fogel suggested, "killing."[8]

Abbott was convicted of first-degree manslaughter instead of the original charge of second-degree murder, the jury apparently buying the "state-raised convict" defense. Afterward, Mailer, who approved of the judgment, expressed his displeasure over the prison sentence, which was set at fifteen years to life.

Mailer had testified at the trial for twenty minutes on January 18. He said that he had come to know Gilmore better in writing *The Executioner's Song* through his correspondence with Abbott, also mentioning the letter he had written in support of Jack's release from prison. He was terribly upset about the whole matter, decrying Adan's death but also opposing, in his subsequent clash with the press on the last day of the trial, the possibility of a life sentence for Abbott. "Adan has already been destroyed," he told the mass of angry reporters, many of whom had already convicted Abbott in their reports; "at least let Abbott become a writer."[9] It was absurdly unfortunate that Mailer tried to defend Abbott after the sensational killing, but he was being true to his long-held belief, going back to his second novel, that America's democracy was in danger of fading into fascism. "A democracy," he insisted, "involves taking risks." The entire session with the press finally boiled over when one of the reporters asked Mailer if he thought Abbott could be safely be released again in a few years instead of giving him life, and Mailer responded in the affirmative. The following day, a photograph of Mailer appeared in the press, showing him holding up for ridicule the front page of the *New York Post* with the headline, "I'd help the killer again."[10]

In actuality, Norman Mailer felt guilty as hell about the whole matter, which ended in the death of another promising artist. "Freedom given to one talented writer resulted in the death of another young, attractive, and gifted man." In an undated handwritten note, he wrote: "I didn't want to speak on this matter but it's getting out of hand. Nobody concerned with getting Abbott out of jail, notably Bob Silver, Erroll McDonald nor myself did it in the spirit of radical chic. We were heavy with responsibility, I promise you." He went on to say that they all knew that they were taking a "calculated risk." They were holding their breath, and "Abbott, I can say, was holding his, too."[11]

16

The *60 Minutes* Interview

When he interviewed Jack Abbott for the television program *60 Minutes*, Ed Bradley was in his first year with the popular CBS news show. He had begun as a reporter for the network in Vietnam, where he was wounded by shrapnel from a mortar round. Bradley was one of the last American newsmen to leave Saigon before its fall in 1975. His vivid reporting there had led to his becoming a White House correspondent during the Carter years and, afterward, one of the regulars on the CBS *Evening News* and anchor on Sundays.[1] The *60 Minutes* interview took place in a federal detention center in Brooklyn and was first aired April 18, 1982. The previous January, Abbott had been convicted of first-degree manslaughter. He was in U.S. custody at the time of the interview because he would first have to finish out his federal sentence for violating his parole before serving the prison sentence in the state of New York. In the original airing in 1982, Bradley opened with the street sounds of jackhammers and sirens in the background:

> Jack Abbott was sentenced to fifteen years to life for murder. Jack Abbott, who had written a book about life in

prison called *In the Belly of the Beast.* He was in prison because he was a killer, the kind of killer about whom many people say, "Lock him up and throw away the key." About the only people we know who were not saying that were a group of prominent authors led by Norman Mailer, who had read his book and were so impressed that they decided to go to bat for Abbott with his parole board. Their intervention helped Abbott to walk out of prison to a hero's welcome of sorts, a party in his honor thrown by the senior editor of one of the country's biggest and most prestigious publishing houses. Shortly after, the group at the dinner party woke up to the news that Jack Abbott had stabbed a young man named Richard Adan to death outside a restaurant in Manhattan's Lower East Side.

In the re-airing of the interview on February 17, 2002, exactly a week after Abbott's death, Bradley opened retrospectively: "A story we reported twenty years ago came back into the news this week. It came back in an item about a misfit named Jack Abbott, who had spent most of his life behind bars and was found dead, hanging in his prison cell. Authorities there say it was a suicide." Before running the 1982 clip, Bradley rehearsed Mailer's role in gaining the killer's release, blaming Mailer in addition to (but not naming) Jason Epstein, editor in chief of Random House, who had given Abbott "a hero's welcome of sorts" in the form of a literary dinner. Turning to the image of Abbott, as the 1982 film began rolling, he recalled in a voice-over that the convict-writer had "claimed to us and to anybody else who would listen" that the fifteen-year-to-life sentence he had received in the Adan stabbing was too harsh. Essentially, the original interview that followed made Abbott look somewhat heartless for trying to dismiss Adan's death as simply an "accident," for which he took no legal responsibility.

Apparently, on the night of the stabbing, Abbott, as we have read, had asked to use the restaurant bathroom, which was reserved for employees. Although Abbott later insisted to Mailer that he had not asked to use the bathroom at the Binibon, he did not argue that point with Bradley. Rather, he said that when Adan had invited him to use the alley outside the restaurant, he suspected that he was being lured outside to fight. "There was no argument," Bradley observed in a voice-over. "Adan led him outside, where male customers urinate next to this Dumpster. Adan watched the street to ensure Abbott's privacy." Speaking in a low Western drawl, Abbott said that even though he ultimately realized Adan was merely looking out for his privacy, he still didn't trust him, thinking that the restaurant manager was possibly looking for witnesses in case there was a fight. When Adan rushed in to tell him that pedestrians were approaching, Abbott claimed he thought he had a knife.

"After I stabbed him," he told Bradley, "he started walking backwards." Abbott said he reached for Adan's shoulders to steady the wounded man, but he couldn't bring himself to touch his victim. "He was making a lot of gurgling sounds in his throat," Abbott added. By this time, both men were on Second Avenue, staring at each other, though in fact it was already a case of the dead staring at the living. Abbott stabbed Adan from behind, as one witness recounted during his trial. When Adan finally collapsed, Abbott said he was dazed: "I remember seeing a-a-a big river of blood shoot at a high velocity, you know, out from—from where he was laying face down into the gutter, and I knew he was dead. And I had—you know, 'I have to run.'"

He ran, he said, because he had to "protect" himself. He couldn't, he said, "rely on shouting or any bystanders to come and help me; I don't rely on the police to come help me. I try to defend myself. I have to." It didn't occur to him after nearly twenty years in prison "to live any other way." The whole thing, he said, had been a "misunderstanding." Here, the camera shifted to Henry Howard, the victim's father-in-law, who asked Bradley rhetorically how in the world he could have possibly gone home that fateful night and told his stepdaughter Ricci that her husband was dead because of a "misunderstanding." When he had screamed at Abbott in court, calling the accused "scum and filth," Howard recalled that Abbott had retorted, "Go write a book." The implication here was that the writer is above the law, as is the existential hipster in Mailer's essay "The White Negro." "That's really in the league with Norman Mailer," Howard told Bradley in the interview. "If you write a book, you're OK; you don't have to obey the law."[2]

As James Atlas stated in *The New Republic* in his criticism of Mailer's involvement shortly before Abbott's trial, the writer embodies some of the traits of the criminal, "who, by giving into impulses the more timid writer can only hope to reenact in his work, is the true artist." For decades, Atlas noted, Mailer had championed this artist, this outlier, in such works as *Advertisements for Myself* (1959) and *An American Dream* (1965), where the protagonist commits murder with impunity. He had embraced another criminal in *The Executioner's Song*, but, until Abbott, he had never actually known or met the condemned "criminal-artist." "Abbott, however, [had] brought him closer to the experience he finds embodied in the criminal—no doubt far closer than he would have wished."[3]

At the time of the trial, Mailer was attacked in the press for continuing to shock the public with his general behavior, a record that included not only the Abbott affair but also, as was noted by almost everyone, his having stabbed his second wife. Right after the Adan stabbing and before Abbott's trial, the September 9, 1981, cover illustration of *The New Republic* had depicted Mailer and Abbott sitting at a table in a restaurant displaying a blood-smeared knife and an open handcuff. Above Mailer's image is a thought bubble with a picture of Sartre and his prison protégé Jean Genet, the petty criminal who became a writer with the philosopher's support. The same issue carried a full-bore denunciation of Abbott's book as "a hectic screed full of shrill political jargon," arguing as well that Mailer had no business suggesting Abbott could have made a living on the outside as a writer.[4]

Under an editorial entitled "The Poetic License to Kill," *Time* magazine complained that the law was skewed when the jury had chosen manslaughter instead of murder in convicting Abbott, because he had been a state-raised convict: "It began to seem that it was not Abbott and his admitted homicide that were on trial but, in a vague and sloppy way, the entire American criminal justice system." And amid the "travesty and pathos" of everything, Mailer had further muddied the waters by positing the idea that the writer, or the artist, was entitled to "a special dispensation." The editorial reviewed the history of the artist, who, for centuries, until the Romantic period had been regarded as merely a "servant" to the church or aristocratic courts. With the advent of Romanticism's theory of nature as the emblem of God and the idea that the artist alone can render nature's divine message, the writer became a demigod of sorts, one who, in Ralph Waldo Emerson's words in "The Poet," could not only *see* God in nature but also report back that conversation to lesser folk in the form of a poem or painting. According to these tenets, the artist was somehow above the law. The magazine quoted Oscar Wilde, who observed: "The fact of a man's being a poisoner is nothing against his prose." "The Mailer doctrine," the editorial concluded, "suggests that somehow the law should set up separate standards for artists"—perhaps, instead of a grand jury, a "panel of literary judges to meet the first Monday at Elaine's in Manhattan," a popular restaurant on the Upper East Side for writers and other celebrities.[5]

With Howard back on camera, Bradley turned to the nature versus nurture issue in Jack's case and asked the victim's father-in-law about the misery of the killer's life—"a man who spent twenty-five of his years locked up one way or another, fourteen of those in solitary confinement—does he alone bear that responsibility for what happened?" Although Howard demurred, he agreed that prisons don't work, that they punish rather than reform—"So there's lots of people accountable for this." Yet he had no kind words for Abbott's case, saying that the Adan and Howard families had "thrown open their lives" after the killing because they wanted full accountability. "Jack Abbott is garbage," he said. "I'm sorry to say it. It didn't work. He is garbage. He has been irreparably harmed by the state. There is nothing we can do about it except lock him up and make *us* safe for the rest of our lives."

Bradley, in asking just who was responsible for irreparably harming Abbott, went through a litany of those who had failed Jack: his parents, the foster homes, juvenile detention at nine years of age, the prisons, the writers, and namely Mailer—who essentially excused Abbott's crimes on the basis of his artistic talent—and, finally, "Jack himself. Jack by his own admission had more violent incidents on his prison record than any other convict."

ABBOTT: I went to prison with a sentence of less than one year and no more than a five-year maximum and ended up spending nineteen years inside for that. They said I was crazy. I don't know. They would say that I was unruly. They would say I was obnoxious. They would say that I was always looking for trouble.

BRADLEY: But you *were* a troublemaker.

ABBOTT: No, I wasn't. They'll tell you I was, but I wasn't a troublemaker. They were the troublemakers. You know, they started the trouble . . . The way they used to make you sit on the wall all night. If you fell down, they'd kick you back up the wall. And that right there. You can't call that discipline to me. That's lookin' for trouble because I—I wouldn't do it!

BRADLEY: How old were you then?

ABBOTT: I don't know. I was—I guess you could say I was in my adolescent years.

BRADLEY: Thirteen, fourteen years old?

ABBOTT: Yeah.

BRADLEY: . . . Norman Mailer, the man who wanted Abbott out of prison.

MAILER: You take an animal that's in the wild, you put him in a cage and keep him in a cage for many, many years, and that animal does not look like animals that are out in the—in the brush. And so, of course, whatever—whether Jack is the original seed of evil, whether Jack is a victim of his environment—and that's a question that's too deep for me to answer—that there's no question that whatever Jack is, he was made much, much worse by all those years in prison.

The attorney Leonard Munker, who had defended Abbott in a previous prison case, was brought on camera at this juncture to confirm Jack's prison paranoia and to state that he should have never been released after so many years in jail, from such a young age.

There followed footage of the Marion compound, Utah State Prison, and Mailer at the press conference after the trial pleading for a shorter sentence for Jack Abbott the artist. "In order to save this country's honor and integrity," he says, "we're willing to gamble with the nuclear future of the world, correct? So, yes, I'm willing to gamble with the safety of certain elements of society to save this man's talent."

"So with Mailer's help," the Bradley voice-over continued, "Abbott was released to a halfway house on New York's Lower East Side, where Jack Abbott claims shootings and stabbings were not uncommon." Turning to the prisoner, Bradley asked Abbott what kind of a world he thought he had stepped into "when you went outside with a man you thought was threatening you . . . He had no weapon. He thought you wanted to urinate." Abbott and Bradley then argued just how dangerous the Lower East Side was then, with Bradley citing friends who lived there without incident—at least without ever having to kill anyone. There is no question, Bradley asserted, that it was a "tough neighborhood . . . but what I'm saying [is] there are other ways to deal with it." Other people, he added, might not have been threatened—to which Abbott objects rather violently: "No. That's what I'm telling you—that it wasn't no—it wasn't paranoid [*sic*]. If somebody tells you, 'Let's go outside,' that's a threat."

At this point, Howard reappeared on camera to ask why Jack was let out of prison. "What was the deal he made at Marion Penitentiary? Who did he blow the whistle on? Who agreed to let him out on the street from solitary confinement, a man who was in prison all his life, who had murdered three [*sic*] men?" Bradley answered Howard's question by saying that the deal Abbott made to get out of Marion "was one he swore [to Mailer and others] he would never make. In 1981, after the longest strike in federal prison history, Jack Abbott, who had been one of the strike's most vocal supporters, cooperated with US attorneys and prison authorities," identifying its leaders.

Here the camera shifted back to Abbott, who is asked what he faces when he goes back to prison.

ABBOTT: What faces me?

BRADLEY: Yeah.

ABBOTT: Probably the rest of my life, *short*.

BRADLEY: Because the guards will be after you? Because the inmates will be after you?

ABBOTT: It's the same thing. They're going to use this—the snitching thing to—make it seem to the inmates that they're doing it because I'm a snitch. That's what they're going to think. What they don't know is that the guards have set that whole situation up.

Here Mailer reappeared in a clip from the news conference following the trial, recommending mercy for Abbott, saying that Adan has already been destroyed. "The only way that—that we, as a—can ever get anything out of this is—out of that tragedy that Richard Adan and his family have gone through, that at least Abbott become a writer." Howard is brought back on stage to answer Bradley's question as to what he would now say to Mailer. Answering, with obvious sarcasm, Howard tells Bradley, "Norman, I love you. I love you for your lack of responsibility. I love you for putting the artist above humanity." Turning back to Mailer, now on the *60 Minutes* program proper, Bradley tells him that the Howards feel that he is partly responsible for Abbott's crime against their son-in-law. "Yeah. I think I'm partially responsible," Mailer answered. "Ah, I think a lot of people are partially responsible, and I'm the foremost of them . . . It's obviously something I'm going to carry for the rest of my life."

With that, the program approached its close with Bradley turning back to Abbott and asking him what his punishment should be.

BRADLEY: You said that a [prison] warden, a Hitler, a Nixon, they must pay.

ABBOTT: Yeah.

BRADLEY: Jack Abbott killed a man. He must pay.

ABBOTT: No.

BRADLEY: Now what do you think you deserve to pay, if anything?

ABBOTT: Wait a minute, wait a minute! Now you—you're telling me that if you're—if you accidentally killed someone, you have to pay. And we're talking about the law; you're talking about my soul. If you're talking about the law, you're wrong. If you're talking about my soul, it's none of your [censored] business. You see what I mean? What I—my remorse is my remorse, and no—you're not going to take it away from me on television.

In their final exchange, Abbott once again insisted that he had committed no crime in the eyes of the law, except possibly "reckless endangerment." He did, however, in alluding to his remorse, concede that he had probably committed an offense in the eyes of Adan's wife and family.

The interview concluded with Bradley's saying that Abbott, with five years remaining on his federal sentence and facing a state sentence of fifteen to life, probably wouldn't be free for at least another twenty years. Later reflecting on the interview, Bradley recalled feeling nervous during it because, he said, "Jack Henry Abbott was a killer who once while in prison had taken a pen and stabbed a doctor in the nose. And at one point, he picked up my pen. So what's going to stop him from doing it again?" Bradley braced himself, he recalled, "sitting on the edge of the chair, weight evenly distributed on both feet so I could move in either direction. If he made a move I was ready to make a move."[6]

Sadly, Bradley never brought up *In the Belly of the Beast* during the interview, except to say it was the reason Mailer and others had lobbied to have its author freed. He did, of course, take up with Henry Howard its cry of the prisoner who was nearly born in captivity. But nothing was said in the exchange about the horrible prison conditions Abbott so forcefully wrote about. Rather, the focus was on Jack's "prison paranoia," to reaffirm that somebody who hadn't spent his life in prison would have dealt differently with the threat Abbott thought Adan posed when he asked him to step outside. In other words, Bradley, an astute and experienced interviewer, subtly suggested in the exchange over the actual dangers of the Lower East Side that Abbott was "innocent" because of "prison paranoia." His closing, though, reaffirmed Howard's conclusion that Abbott was regrettably "damaged goods" and should have never been allowed out of prison.

17

His Grandmother's Orchard

Mailer opened *The Executioner's Song* with a tantalizing allusion to the book of Genesis. Brenda and Gary, six and seven years old, play in the garden of their grandmother. Falling from a limb that breaks at the top of an apple tree, Brenda lands in Gary's arms. "They were scared," Mailer writes. "The apple trees were their grandmother's best crop and it was forbidden to climb the orchard. [Brenda] helped him drag away the tree limb and they hoped no one would notice." They heard no voice in the garden, but Gary Gilmore had committed his first "crime," had taken his first step in the recurrent cycle of the fall of man. The next time Brenda saw her cousin, Gary was thirteen and had already entered reform school.

We have no record of Jack Abbott as a child. Only Abbott himself was left to tell, or remember, and the story he told Mailer has few references to the period before his early incarceration—indeed, a time so remote in Jack's life that he probably couldn't have remembered that much of it. Once when Mailer, perhaps facetiously, referred to his correspondent's life as a "saga," Abbott lashed out at him for even suggesting there was any lightness or humor to his biography. As far as he was concerned, his life in prison was no romance but, rather, a metaphor for the human condition. Talent had redeemed him but only briefly, and so he was unable to transform himself by turning his life into art. Feeling that he had been convicted in the press rather than in the courtroom, he was now on his way back to the only life he would ever know. He would first go to Marion to finish his federal sentence and then to a series of state prisons in New York for the killing of another artist, Richard Adan. Jack went back to jail, and his book kept selling.

Henry Howard and his stepdaughter Ricci hired F. Lee Bailey to persuade a New York Supreme Court justice to freeze Abbott's royalties, which then amounted to about fifty thousand dollars being held in escrow. Before Abbott's trial, Mailer had warned him to make provisions to settle with Adan's wife in a suit, but Abbott was afraid it would undercut his plea of not guilty. Ricci, who was later awarded $7.5 million in damages in a wrongful death suit in civil court, considered another lawsuit against the parole authorities that had released Abbott from prison six weeks before the killing. According to Bailey, the litigation was necessary. "It's about time to face the fact that some prisoners should never be released," he said. "Abbott, for example, is an unsalvageable person." The true culprit in the mind of Howard, who had been barred from the trial for loudly denouncing Abbott in court, was not Mailer or the others who had written to the parole board on Jack's behalf, but prison professionals, who should have known better than a writer of fiction when it came to weighing the chances of success in freeing somebody from a life of incarceration with a record as violent as Abbott's. Mailer was scorned for his support of Abbott, both before the killing, when he lobbied for Abbott's release, and afterward, when he spoke out against the prison sentence following Jack's conviction. Ricci's mother, Luisa Howard, had taught literature in the Philippines and considered Mailer a literary genius. But now she questioned his lack of sensitivity. The Howards also blamed Mailer and Jean Malaquais, who attended the trial as well, for influencing a verdict that allowed the possibility that Jack might one day walk out of prison again. "How can you sit there and influence the jury?" Howard asked the seventy-three-year-old Malaquais during a break in the trial. "Are you so old that you're crazy? In your daughter's lifetime Abbott is going to be back on the streets with a knife."[1]

In using his influence as a noted writer to get Jack out of prison, Mailer had made a mistake, the second great error of his life. The first had been the stabbing of Adele. After the trial, he had argued not for Abbott's immediate freedom but for the possibility of his being free after serving four or five years for the Adan stabbing. Otherwise, he was just sad about the whole matter, numbed into silence. Mailer went on with his life as a writer, eventually making an extended trip to the Soviet Union in 1995 for a book that would become *Oswald's Tale: An American Mystery*. Lee Harvey Oswald was another mystery, and Mailer's opinion of him confirms Luisa Howard's sense of the writer's occasional insensitivity. Mailer concludes *Oswald's Tale* by comparing Oswald's life to that of Clyde Griffiths in *An American Tragedy*. "Who among us," he concludes, "can say that [Oswald] is in no way related to our own dream? If it had not been for Theodore Dreiser and his last great work, one would like to have used 'An American Tragedy' as the title for this journey through Oswald's beleaguered life." This, of course, is the Mailer of "The White Negro," the writer who celebrates the social outlier. He elevates the rebel and the gangster, who in his romance of America become heroes.

The correspondence between Abbott and Mailer resumed in 1982. Mailer, who was then finishing *Ancient Evenings*, was impressed by the amount of reading Jack was doing since he had been put back behind bars and, along with Robert Silvers of the *NYRB*, sent him books from time to time. "I feel—I hope I'm right," he told Jack in a fit of wishful thinking dated December 20, "that you may be at the beginning of some years of serious writing, and who knows, after the experience of the last twelve months . . . maybe once you have gone through the endless labors of digesting these profound highs and lows, well maybe you'll be writing better than ever." When not sharing philosophical ideas with Mailer, Abbott would rehearse over and over the fading details of his encounter with Adan and the time he had spent on the lam.

That's all that was left to him, in fact: the death of Richard Adan and his life as a prisoner. It was karma. He would go to prison with the hope of getting out and then kill to remain there. It was a cycle begun with the killing of Christensen, and its latest revolution had ended with the killing of Adan. His original offense was to have been "born into" prison. Going there as a preteen and teenager had simply ruined his chances of avoiding the worst of the human condition—crime and punishment. The pattern repeats itself every year in America, mainly with impoverished children and particularly with impoverished black males, whose middle-class counterparts, those perhaps who have been assisted by affirmative action programs, are nevertheless in danger of being arrested for "driving while black."

In 2014 there were numerous reported cases of the mistreatment of teenage prisoners at Rikers Island in New York City. In one case, a sixteen-year-old black male spent more than three years awaiting trial on charges that were ultimately withdrawn. He missed his last two and a half years of high school and entered the job market as an "ex-con" because he had been on probation for another offense when charged with the one that put him away. He was no devil, simply a youth in the kind of bad company that arises from economic and social inequality. If he had been middle-class, his parents could have afforded the $3,000 bail and thus spared their son irreversible psychic damage.

Inside the prison, investigative reporter Jennifer Gonnerman writes, Kalief Browder "was assigned to a dorm where about fifty teenage boys slept in an open room, each with a plastic bucket to store his possessions in." To get their clothes cleaned, they were required to wash them themselves in the bucket holding their possessions. "The dayroom was ruled over by a gang leader and his friends, who controlled inmates' access to the prison phones and dictated who could sit on a bench to watch TV and who had to sit on the floor." His court-appointed attorney never visited him at Rikers, claiming only that he may have done one teleconference. "For the defendant who is in jail, the more a case drags on the greater the pressure to give up and plead guilty." Browder persisted in declaring his innocence, delay after delay, as he appeared before as many as eight different judges, probably having no idea of how few defendants ever actually get to trial instead of plea bargaining. "In 2011 in the Bronx," Gonnerman writes, "only a hundred and sixty-five cases went to trial; in three thousand nine hundred and ninety-one cases, the defendant pleaded guilty."[2]

Browder attempted suicide several times, but he never took a plea bargain, even when the sentence was "time served." On three or four occasions, he spent long periods in solitary confinement—at Rikers, it was called the Central Punitive Segregation Unit, known to everyone as the Bing, which contained four hundred twelve-by-seven-foot cells. Part of the scandal unveiled at Rikers in 2014 dealt with the excessive use of punitive segregation. Between 2007 and 2012, its use was increased by more than 60 percent—made the more noxious by the noise and fumes coming from adjacent LaGuardia International Airport and the lack of air-conditioning in the prison. When he was finally released, he came home a changed person. He stayed, and paced, in his room much as he had paced in solitary. Just being around more than one person felt strange to him. He had little in common by then with his school friends, many of whom had graduated and gotten on with their lives. "Being home is way better than being in jail," he told Gonnerman. "But in my mind right now I feel like I'm still in jail because I'm still feeling the side effects from what happened there."[3]

Browder, a teenager and thus much more vulnerable than an adult prisoner, did not survive the psychic damage of prison. In June 2015, at the age of twenty-two, he committed suicide.[4] Jack

Abbott was subjected to such cruel conditions in both adolescence and adulthood before *he* was finally released from prison. Solitary confinement in his teen years surely left its mark on him, "a profound spiritual effect," as he wrote in *In the Belly of the Beast*. "I suffered from *claustrophobia* for years when I first went to prison. I never knew any form of suffering more horrible in my life." The air in the cramped cell seemed to vanish: "You are smothering. Your eyes bulge out; you clutch at your throat; you scream like a banshee. Your arms flail the air in your cell. You reel about the cell, falling." Claustrophobically, the walls "press you from all directions with an invisible force . . . You become hollow and empty. Dying a hard death. One that lingers and toys with you." He developed an anger that wouldn't relent, even in freedom. *In the Belly of the Beast* contains yet another passage about cell space that is alarmingly profound. "Let us say you are in a cell ten feet long and seven feet wide. That means seventy feet of *floor* space. But your bunk is just over three feet wide and six and a half feet long. Your iron toilet and sink combination covers a floor space of at least three feet by two feet. All tallied, you have approximately forty-seven square feet of space on the floor. It works out to a pathway seven feet long and about three feet wide." If an animal in a zoo were housed in the same cramped space, he concludes, "the Humane Society would have the zookeeper arrested for cruelty."[5] In other words, it should be illegal to confine any sort of animal to such a small space.

Now back in prison following the summer of 1981 and his 1982 conviction, Jack seemed to have lost his thirst for that freedom.

Temporarily, at least. He still wanted to be free, but after the odyssey of the previous year, he appeared to be taking advantage of being back in prison—where he could think and *write*, something he hadn't done very much of in the "free world." His engagement with writing fiction, however, soon morphed into another rehash of the night he stabbed Adan, a sign that he was perhaps already thinking about his 1987 book, which contains a play about that fatal night and would be entitled, ever so painfully, *My Return*. Along the way, he may have become disheartened. While in solitary, he had tried to hang himself, after writing a sixty-page letter to Mailer, one that is now apparently lost. He told his mentor in a letter of June 1 that he made a noose "from the heavy material in a mattress" and tied it to a light fixture. Standing on his tiptoes, he wound the other end tightly around his neck. "As I was blacking out I'd always get back up on my toes and desperately unwind the rope I fashioned around my neck. It was my *body* struggling against me to stay alive. I must have done this a dozen times." Perhaps he described here the way he would kill himself in 2002—if in fact he committed suicide and was not killed by other inmates. As noted earlier, officials at the Wende Correctional Facility in Alden, New York, stated that he left a suicide note. That note, however, has never been released to the public. This author's letter of inquiry was never answered.

Following the conclusion of his trial in the winter of 1982, Jack mainly alternated between writing confessional letters to Mailer, in which he contritely admitted his inability after so many years in prison to have an intimate relationship with anyone (though he would later marry Naomi Zack), and ranting about Majeski, the policeman who was credited with his capture. By this time, he was headed back to finish his federal prison sentence before doing the New York time for manslaughter and was being held at the federal jail in Otisville, New York. He resented the fact that Mailer and Majeski had become friends after the capture and trial. (In fact, Majeski would go on to help Mailer research the American side of his 1995 *Oswald's Tale.*) "God, Norman, *anyone* can look at Majeski and see what's happening with him. Oh, he wants so badly for me to call him the little asshole he is—'the hunted and the big bad Hunter!' Ha-ha! Wow, I can't believe you'd go for that, Norman."[6]

"I'm sorry I did this to you," Abbott told him, referring to the Adan stabbing. "You know that. There are too many 'ifs' to wish for, from the beginning of my life, it seems . . . so many wrong turns." If he could get "a little peace," he hoped to write about it clearly now. "I was so bitter when I walked out of prison," he added. He recalled the bitterness bubbling over when he stood in front of his mother's grave in Salt Lake City with his sister. Later, everywhere he went, "I was the author of that book and it killed me, that is why I never wanted to talk about prison or see anyone that reminded me of prison." Meanwhile, he feared going back to Marion, where he had given authorities a "statement" in order to facilitate his 1981 release. On July 14, 1982, he described the harassment he faced at the Otisville unit. The authorities knew "nothing" about the need to protect him from other inmates, either there or at Marion, where he had requested to be placed in protective custody. Inmates shouted at him "24 hours a day. Each time the guards would come to my door to take me to one of the routine appearances before the administrative staff, they would strip me nude and then run a metal detector over my body." With Abbott's record of two fatal knifings, nobody was taking any chances. "They would carefully search my trousers and tee-shirt." Once back in his clothes, he was handcuffed from behind and forced, he said, "to walk up the prison corridor around other inmates who were passing back and forth." He heard their talk, their accusations that he had been a "snitch" at Marion. He vowed to fight to the end to protect himself. "I know one thing now, they'll have to *take* me out," he told Mailer on July 24. "There will be no *suicide*."

Instead of Marion, he was first sent to the federal prison in Springfield, Missouri, which specialized in mentally deranged prisoners. Jack was included because of a suspected suicide attempt. As a safety precaution, he was allowed to read only paperback books. He wasn't crazy, he said. It was just another way for prison authorities to punish him. He now said that he accepted his imprisonment for killing Adan, but he didn't want it to last a lifetime. During the *60 Minutes* interview, he had even come close to admitting remorse for the stabbing, not simply regret that it had happened and landed him back in jail. No violence was ever acceptable—in a perfect world. "It is pardonable, however, in a world of human beings who . . . are subject to accidents and misunderstandings as long as they live."[7] This was in a letter to Larry Flynt, publisher of *Penthouse*. The magazine had published an interview that it had conducted in June with Abbott under the title, "Explosive Interview with Murderer Jack Henry Abbott."

Abbott had apparently seen a draft of the article, which appeared in the December 1982 issue, and wanted Flynt to tone it down. He didn't, as the title makes clear. Peter Manso, a friend of Mailer's, conducted the interview and later used some of the material in his book on Mailer's life up to that time.

In this interview, Abbott explained why other prisoners might have resented *In the Belly of the Beast*: "because I said some things that are very painful for an inmate to realize." Only white inmates felt that way, he added. "The black inmates, they like it. Mexicans like it; Puerto Ricans like it."[8] Asked why blacks liked his book, Abbott answered that prison was simply a part of their society since "one out of every six" blacks had done time. Prison, therefore, was socially acceptable; whereas for white ex-cons, it meant becoming ostracized. *In the Belly of the Beast* was painful for whites because it undercut the basic dignity whites felt for simply being white in a multiethnic society. In his earliest letters to Mailer, long before his 1981 release and return to prison, Abbott had spoken nostalgically of the "good convict." He was a white man who stood his ground and claimed his manhood in an environment where manhood was forbidden for prisoners. Abbott, like Gilmore, was a child of the 1950s and early sixties, when prisons were either largely white or segregated. Later, white prisoners became the new "niggers." The effects of the civil rights movement further undercut their sense of dignity, since they were not as well protected by the new order as were blacks, at least they didn't think so.

18

Jack's Return

Back in prison, Jack was initially occupied with several issues. He was both infuriated and disappointed when the *National Guardian*, a radical leftist weekly newspaper, agreed with his conviction for first-degree manslaughter, ignoring his defense that the stabbing had been an accident. More painful was the fact that the author of the *Guardian* piece was Akinshiju C. Ola, a radical leftist writer who had actually served time with Abbott in Marion in the late 1970s. While still at the Brooklyn House of Detention in January 1982, following his conviction but before his sentencing, which came that spring, Abbott constructed a nearly fifty-page typewritten document (dated January 20) in which he denounced the radical newspaper for echoing the verdict of "the lower courts of the reptile American Press." Since his capture, he said, he had refused all requests for interviews from the American press, hoping that the communist or Marxist press would come to his aid with an interview request. In fact, the *National Guardian* was on its last legs and would fold in 1992, having existed since the 1940s with the birth of the Progressive Party and the 1948 presidential campaign of Henry Wallace. Stalinism, even Maoism, had largely disappeared from American political thought by the 1980s. Jack hadn't perhaps fully realized it because he'd been in prison.

Ola had apparently alluded to Abbott's so-called betrayal of the progressive lawyers at Marion, lawyers who, Abbott said, subsisted on funds not only from the federal government but also the Catholic Church. Although admitting to the charge of "betrayal," or snitching, he scowled at the idea that any self-respecting Marxist would defend an "alliance" with the Church. In his opinion, such attorneys merely used prisoners to gain publicity and further their own political or professional ambitions, which ultimately aligned them with the prison administration, not the prisoners. Ola dismissed Abbott as a common criminal instead of a revolutionary, suggesting that he lacked the commitment of an Eldridge Cleaver or a George Jackson. As a result, Abbott was effectively reduced, after twenty-five years in prison, to the status of only a "convict/rebel" who had agreed to inform against progressive lawyers in order to gain his parole from Marion. In defense, Abbott noted that the Marion prisoners' strike proceeded even after the lawyers were exposed.

Abbott felt as if he had been left behind in the quest for prison reformation solely because of his race. "What is noteworthy here," Abbott wrote, "is *why* left-communists in America *instinctively* consider all white prisoners (e.g., white proletarians) a dangerous threat to their positions of control over The Movement, namely: Influence over non-white comrades in the national liberation organizations."[1] Ola, who incidentally died in the same week in 2002 as Abbott, was black. A native of New Orleans, he had been active—according to his obituary in the *New York Amsterdam News,* one of the nation's oldest black newspapers—"on both musical and political fronts . . . He was a member of an organization that pushed the Civil Rights Movement to the left . . . before he was charged with passing bad checks to secure arms." While serving time at Marion, "he began his writing career, earning the respect of fellow inmates and officials. Once on the streets in the late 70's he became an advocate for prison reform."[2] Even though Jack's *Guardian* antagonist channeled his efforts through radical groups like the Black Liberation Army, Abbott would have been pained and angered to receive criticism from somebody like Ola, an advocate for prison reform. He resented being dismissed from the revolution as a traitor for ratting on progressive lawyers.

It was a tempest in a teapot to anybody outside the "movement" and prison. Even Mailer thought less of Abbott after learning of his snitching at Marion. "I didn't know," he fibbed, "when Abbott got out of jail and discovered—I can't believe it—in the piece Robert Sam Anson did for *Life* magazine, was that his release from prison came about because he turned in other prisoners . . . I think Abbott came out with prodigious bad conscience, because he's a proud fellow and must always be right in everything he does. I can't begin to contemplate the state of confusion he was living in."[3] Mailer had suspected Jack's snitching, and now he was pulling back from his former protégé.

Abbott was further wounded when, in the summer of 1982, while he was then confined in Otisville, Mailer questioned whether

Jack truly ever believed that Adan had possessed a knife during their confrontation. (The knife was apparently never found.) The "accusation," he said, was still ringing in his ears, getting "louder and more vicious, more maddening, as time passes." He felt that he had been let down by everybody—even his attorney, Ivan Fisher, who "was misrepresenting me and in effect cooperating with the DA." But the biggest blow was Mailer's backsliding. As Abbott wrote to Mailer, it felt as if "you were trading me in for Majeski to amuse yourself now that your 'exceptional nigger' had reverted to his slum ways."[4]

Mailer's growing reticence about Abbott was showing. He was apparently weighing his anger against Jack for screwing up against his fading belief that the artist in Abbott still deserved saving. He was also becoming more and more impatient of Abbott's paranoia as well as the hopelessness of the convict's situation. At first, he tried to encourage Jack's writing, even in the face of so much more prison time, but before long he had to confess that he hardly knew what to say to the prisoner. The tension would eventually doom their epistolary friendship.

Mailer's many correspondents at this time also included two other friends in trouble with the law, both of whom would spend time in prison: Bernard "Buzz" Farber, an editor Mailer had known since the 1960s and one of his "two or three best friends," and Richard Stratton, a filmmaker Mailer had known for even longer. Both were convicted of selling drugs (in Stratton's case, cannabis) and confined to federal prisons—Farber for nearly four years, and

Stratton, as the ringleader of the illegal operation, for eight. When the feds arrested Farber and Stratton, they suspected that their friend Mailer was somehow involved and set out to include him in their sting operation. They arranged an interview between Farber, wearing a wire, and Mailer, in spite of the fact that Farber had consistently maintained that Mailer was in no way involved. To please the feds and possibly reduce his prison sentence, he went ahead with the interview, expecting Mailer to establish his own innocence, which he did.

Even though Farber had involuntarily cooperated with the authorities' attempt to entrap Mailer, he was twice turned down for early parole at the federal prison in Loretto, Pennsylvania, before his release in 1990. His correspondence with Mailer and others carried the same sad irony found in Abbott's prison letters—the deep lament that neither, though guilty of a crime, deserved incarceration for so long a time. In reporting his first unsuccessful encounter with the parole board, he reported: "After a five minute wait outside, I was called back into the room . . . and told me they would 'see me again March 20th, *1988* for my interim (second) hearing." To underscore their desires, his "case manager" called him in the next day to be certain he understood that his request for parole after serving seven months had been flatly turned down because he continued to refuse to implicate Mailer. The "very next day" he was given duties usually reserved for prisoners who had committed infractions. The disappointment Farber suffered after being turned down for early parole was exacerbated by the warden, who told him in a faux-naïve tone, "39 [more] months is a lot of time for someone 21 or 31. For someone 51 it is extremely difficult." Farber committed suicide not long after he had served his full forty-six months.[5]

Abbott, too, may have ended his life that way, but in 1982 he was full of plans to get himself out of prison long before fifteen more years. Yet the apparent decline of Mailer's interest left Abbott in a bind, to say the least. He had somehow to continue his defense even after his conviction and sentencing. He hadn't simply killed somebody over the use of a bathroom. It was, as he had told Ed Bradley on *60 Minutes*, the result of a "misunderstanding." He would write a second book. Like the first, it would be consumed with the deadly details of his incarceration. The first time around, his complaint was that he had begun his conscious life as a "state-raised convict." If the conviction ultimately wasn't altogether wrong, the length of the sentencing was. Like Billy Budd, whose last words are used in the epigraph to *My Return*, Jack hadn't been responsible in the eyes of God.

Abbott's second book was published in 1987 with the editorial assistance of Naomi Zack. Following Jack's trial in New York City, Zack believed that Abbott had been railroaded and set out to include him in a documentary on crime victims and the criminal justice system. As the jacket for *My Return* notes of Zack: "She is convinced that Abbott was unfairly convicted by an outraged public opinion inflamed by sensational treatment in the media." In 1986, Zack, a graduate of Columbia University with a doctorate in philosophy, moved to Plattsburg, New York, where Abbott was first held once he had finished the remainder of his federal sentence. He was returned to serve his state sentence of fifteen years to life at the Clinton Correction Facility in Dannemora, in New York near the Canadian border and known as "Little Siberia." During the period in which Abbott was working on *My Return*, Zack visited him every day, provided him with the books he required, conveyed his messages, and typed his manuscript. She evidently remained in Plattsburg until 1992, when she divorced Abbott after two years of marriage.[6]

Even while becoming discouraged about Jack, Mailer continued on occasion to urge him to keep up his writing, but to write about something other than prison. "Maybe the time has come," he suggested in early 1984, "for you to turn to novel writing." The suggestion that he write about something other than prison, even in a novel, was probably unrealistic, because prison was nearly the only life he ever knew, except for his peripatetic childhood and his brief time out in the summer and fall of 1981. But Mailer thought that the "fertility" of Abbott's mind—"your intellectual imagination you might be able to write fantastic novels, surrealistic novels, novels in spaceships . . ." The surreal, the confinement of a spaceship would perhaps lend itself to the restrictions of Jack's imagination and situation. In *My Return*, however, he revisited the reality of his tragic past by reconstructing a play with overly precise stage directions the circumstances of his encounter with Richard Adan. "It seems to me, Jack," Mailer continued, "that you have the gift to be able occasionally . . . to come up with something truly interesting." He cited a lost play Jack had written about five men in solitary "as truly interesting." It was too long and clearly suffered from its author's ignorance about staging a play, but it had "at the same time a grasp of theater, and I was much impressed with that."[7]

The first part of the book consists of the play entitled "The Death of Tragedy," playing off George Steiner's famous 1961 work with the same title. Steiner is a French-born American philosopher, critic, and novelist. Abbott's "The Death of Tragedy" is essentially a plea of temporary insanity that is based on the classic definition of tragedy, in which the fault of the transgressor lies inward and cannot be avoided. In other words, it was simply fate that brought Jack to the Binibon restaurant at 5:00 A.M. on July 18, 1981. That is to say, as Jack insisted during his *60 Minutes* interview, killing Adan had been an accident resulting from a "misunderstanding." It did not result from "some fatality of over-reaching or self-mutilation resulting from a malignancy" (Foreword, Steiner's *The Death of Tragedy*). As Zack writes in her introduction to *My Return*, "At his trial . . . Jack made an effort to doubt the facts [favorable to his defense] by reinterpreting them in such a way as to please [the prosecution] . . . That Jack should doubt himself . . . resulted from habits of thought attributable to Socratic wisdom [i.e., "I know that I do not know," thereby, undercutting his accusers who think they do know when they don't]. It is on that philosophical point that tragedy falls into a farce [because Abbott/Socrates proves himself the wisest]."[8] By taking the position that he doesn't *know*, he turns tragedy to farce, thereby dismissing the trial, in which he felt he was convicted primarily in the press.

By invoking Socratic wisdom and asserting the death of tragedy, Abbott turned his back on both his original defense as a "state-raised convict" and on his primary influence, Karl Marx, who rejected classical tragedy because it placed the blame, however problematically, on the individual rather than society. The double identity of Abbott (ABBOTT and ABBOTT CHARACTER), the one answering questions on the stand as the other becomes drowned in the drama, seems to be sleepwalking through the play, as if drawn, or redrawn, through his final downfall.

Much of *My Return* was probably conceived and possibly even drafted back at Marion federal prison, where in 1982 Abbott was returned to finish his federal term for violating his probation in the killing of Adan. In its "Men of Letters" section, the book reflects the content of Abbott's long letters to Mailer, which he wrote upon his "return" to prison following their unsuccessful experiment to see if art could outweigh criminality. That correspondence consists of extended explanations and arguments over whether he "murdered" Adan; an autobiography relating information about his early life with his parents and time in foster homes, his attachments to the Mormon family whose patriarch was twice imprisoned for plural marriage, and his ultimate conversion to Judaism; and his exegesis of the Torah. When his federal sentence was completed in 1986, he was returned to the state of New York to serve his sentence of fifteen years to life.

This book's appearance also coincided with the end of the correspondence, if not altogether the friendship, between Abbott and Mailer. When Naomi Zack asked Mailer in April 1986 to write an afterword for *My Return*, he refused on the grounds that "it would injure the book." He was referring to the bad press he had recently received from the PEN Congress fiasco, in which, as that year's president, he had invited George Shultz, the secretary of state, to speak, angering the liberal group, but he had other, deeper reasons and signed off with the vague suggestion that he might provide a blurb, if he liked the book. Mailer was done with Jack's paranoia in the wake of his New York trial. He may have read the manuscript of *My Return* before refusing to write the blurb, and if he had read Jack's new book, he would have encountered the same brooding, bickering commentary that had come through the prisoner's letters to him over the last five years. While declining to write an afterword, he recommended Lionel Abel, a translator of Sartre and a frequent contributor to *Partisan Review*. Evidently, Abel also declined, for there *is* no afterword, though Abel is apparently included as one of the addressees in the "Men of Letters" section in the third section of the book (the first consisting of the play; and the second, the "appendix," which features diagrams of the crime scene).[9]

Published by a small press, *My Return* did nothing to help Jack's case. In putting the book together, he hoped it would realize his dream of getting paroled early, but its vindictive tone clearly undercut its effectiveness. It was filled with hostility not only to his manslaughter victim but to all those who had been involved in his "return"—William Majeski, the detective who had organized the manhunt and successful capture; Ivan Fisher, his lawyer, whom he had fired and rehired repeatedly during and after his trial; and prison officials who had humiliated and allegedly beaten him in federal prison, especially in Springfield, where he was held before his return to Marion. The book wasn't reviewed widely, and where it was reviewed the spotlight was on Abbott the "murderer" instead of Abbott the wrongfully accused or Abbott the "state-raised convict."

My Return became the focus of a two-part article in *The Boston Globe* of September 13–14, 1987. Its author, Mark Muro, described Abbott as looking like Lenin ("a hero of his"), and indeed the photograph of him in Muro's piece, looking straight into the camera lens with his heavy mustache and rimless glasses, suggested as much. Entitled "Murder, he wrote, in a bid for freedom," Muro's first installment spoke of Abbott's prison emaciation and green-garbed prison uniform and quoted Abbott as saying from Dannemora: "See, I'm not going to be a prison writer . . . I refuse to be a professional inmate." Sadly, that's practically all that Jack Henry Abbott had ever been. He went on to lament his abandonment by the literary establishment—it had failed to "recognize" the unfairness of his New York trial. Now, he realized he was on his "own." "Living now in a regular cell," Muro wrote, "cell 34, one of 48 on the same tier with David Berkowitz, the Son of Sam serial killer, Jack Abbott exists all 24 of a day's hours either in his isolation cell or with Zack in the visiting room." Interestingly, Abbott had written favorably of Berkowitz in his earlier letters to Mailer.

Describing *My Return* as obsessive, arrogant, and cold, Muro records the angry responses of William Majeski, who described the book as full of "blatant lies," and Henry Howard, who lambasted not only the author but its publisher, Prometheus Books, of Buffalo, New York, as "unscrupulous" for publishing it. Howard's late son-in-law, Muro wrote, is described in the book as "a troublemaker," while Abbott is characterized as simply trying to have breakfast. The innuendo, the outright viciousness of the book's personal attacks, also conflicts with the high ground Abbott tried to take in his "Men of Letters" section. "See," he is quoted in part two of the *Globe* article, "I'm trying to behave like a 'real' intellectual." The second and last installment, entitled "Jack's Letters to Norman," summarizes the story of their correspondence, Abbott's alleged adoption by the "radical chic," and his trial, attended by such movie celebrities as Susan Sarandon and Christopher Walken. Mailer, the main focus of this section, is reported to have refused, through his literary agent, "to speak of the matter."

So there ended essentially the life of Jack Henry Abbott and the legacy of *The Executioner's Song*. Over, too, was the literary friendship that unfortunately led to the violent death of another artist, Richard Adan, dead at twenty-two. Jack lived another sixteen years—in prison—and died on February 10, 2002, nearly three weeks after his fifty-eighth birthday. Shortly before his death (he was found hanging in his cell by a bedsheet and a shoelace tied together), he had been once more rejected in a bid for parole, having already served more than the first fifteen of his fifteen-to-life sentence for first-degree manslaughter. In denying Abbott parole for at least another two years, the board noted that it had been "struck by the absolute lack of any sign of remorse for your fatal actions [in slaying Adan] and no mention of the pain and suffering your extremely violent actions have caused the family of the victim."[10] By that time, he had lost the exotic look of his fugitive days, his face grimly exhibiting the wear and tear of prison life. Like Gilmore (and doubtless many prisoners), he suffered trouble with his teeth, further adding to his early aged countenance. Two years before his death, while being held at the infamous Attica state prison, he had been brutally beaten by other prisoners, inmate revenge that he had feared since being sent back to prison in 1982. "Listen," he wrote Mailer on March 6, 1984, "when I write, I get an outbreak of sweats and a rash all over my body. I read what I wrote the next day and it makes me *physically ill* . . . Those fools want me *murdered* and there is *nothing* I can write that will not be attacked in such a way that will endanger my *life* . . ." If he kept writing, nothing of it has survived, except his letters in the Mailer papers at the University of Texas and those he sent to other mostly unknown correspondents. Whether or not the cause of his death was suicide, its circumstances were very similar to the suicide attempt he had described to Mailer, one in which, he wrote, the body fought against the mind in deadly prison combat. "I am the poet of the Body and I am the poet of the Soul," Walt Whitman wrote in *Leaves of Grass*. For the poet of democracy, the bard of the downtrodden, the two entities were lovers, not enemies, except, as it turned out, in Jack's world.

"His life was tragic from beginning to end," Mailer wrote in a prepared statement to the press. "I never knew a man who had a worse life. What made it doubly awful is that he brought down on one young man full of promise and left a bomb crater of lost possibilities for many, including most especially himself."[11]

Norman Mailer died on November 10, 2007, at the age of

eighty-four. After Jack, he continued to write books, nine more, in fact, sending his onetime literary ward fewer and fewer letters, or responses. In one of them, he excused himself, saying he wasn't writing that many letters to anyone (they took him and his energy away from books, and he would then have to set aside an entire week or so to dictate letters to a variety of people). "Also, in truth," he told him, "I feel a little like a burnt-out case. I hardly knew what to say to you anymore . . . Your letters are obviously showing huge pain and confusion and all kinds of hassles . . ." He realized at a certain point that it would be "a cottage industry" to try to keep replying on equal terms on anything approaching Jack's "insatiable intellectual curiosity."[12]

There had been a rumor afloat that Norman had broken with Abbott "because I thought there was anti-Semitic content" in *In the Belly of the Beast*. He told Sharon Churcher in 1993 that he hadn't seen it really. "There were traces perhaps but then when aren't there?"[13] The rumor had probably started with Jack himself, no doubt desperate to get back into contact with Mailer. On at least one other occasion after killing Adan, he had triggered a quarrel with Mailer in an effort to reboot their flagging correspondence. In 1988 Mailer confessed to Joyce Carol Oates, who may have briefly considered taking up Abbott as a literary subject, that he hadn't corresponded with the prisoner "for the last few years," adding, "I must remind him of one of the worst periods in his life, as he does of a bad one in mine."[14] Oates had recently published *On Boxing*, in which she implied that boxing wasn't a sport because people didn't "play" at it. Neither had either Muhammad Ali or George Foreman in Norman Mailer's *The Fight*. Nor had the "pugilists" in prison combat, where the contest is a dark metaphor for the human condition. It is "war" instead of "peace," where the mortality of life is simply speeded up, as it is in Norman Mailer's *The Executioner's Song*, and—fatefully—Jack Henry Abbott's *In the Belly of the Beast*.

Acknowledgments

In undertaking this book, one of first people I met was J. Michael Lennon, who soon afterward published his astonishingly exhaustive authorized biography of Norman Mailer; a year later, he came out with a selected edition of Mailer's voluminous letters. Both publications have served me well in this stint, as has Mike Lennon's generosity in advising me in my research of the subject and in his careful reading of my manuscript. He doesn't agree with my every point, but on the whole I hope he appreciates my admiration for the author of *The Executioner's Song.*

Once again, Philip McFarland read at least one of my drafts and gave, as usual, his helpful hints. Of my colleagues at Texas A&M University, John J. McDermott of the philosophy department assisted me in interpreting some of Jack Henry Abbott's allusions to philosophers in *My Return*. In the English department, Jeffrey and Jennifer Goodman Wollock helped me locate obscure items online for this book. Others there who helped are William Bedford Clark, Michael Collins, and Charles B. Taylor, Jr. A student IT worker, Agha Abbas, also helped. Without the superb interlibrary loan services of my university under the leadership of

Ms. Zheng Ye Yang, this book would have eaten up a lot of air miles.

My gratitude goes to Gary Fisketjon and Erroll McDonald at Random House for sharing their memories of Jack Abbott. I would also like to acknowledge Robert Silvers of *The New York Review of Books* for his information about the jailhouse author. William J. Majeski, the New York City detective who pursued Abbott relentlessly after he fatally stabbed Richard Adan, both read my manuscript and filled in valuable details about the crime and Abbott's capture. I am also grateful to Ricci Reyes Adan for providing photographs of her late husband and herself for this book. I would like to acknowledge the Harry Ransom Center at the University of Texas at Austin, where the Norman Mailer papers are housed, for its hospitality and resources, especially Pat Fox in the reading room; for permission to publish brief excerpts from Mailer's unpublished letters in the Ransom Center's Humanities Research Center, I thank Susan Mailer, Sam Radin, and the Norman Mailer estate. I am also grateful to James McGrath Morris for giving me a copy of the bound galleys of *In the Belly of the Beast*. For the material from the *60 Minutes* program on which Abbott appeared with Ed Bradley in 1982, I am thankful to Vicki Gordon, senior story editor of the CBS program, for providing a text of the show; my sister Mary Loving, for putting me in contact with Ms. Gordon; and Ann M. Fotiades, for arranging the licensing request.

My agent, Don Fehr, of Trident Media, was enthusiastic from the first about this book. Gratitude as well goes to my editor at

Thomas Dunne Books, Emily Angell. Finally, I want to thank my wife, Cathleen C. Loving, who without complaint has patiently listened, day after day, to my spoken thoughts about any book I write.

Notes

Epigraph

1. "A Murderer's Tale: Norman Mailer Talking to Melvyn Bragg, November 15, 1979," in *Conversations with Norman Mailer*, ed. J. Michael Lennon (Jackson: University Press of Mississippi, 1988), 253.

Introduction

1. *Selected Letters of Norman Mailer*, ed. J. Michael Lennon (New York: Random House, 2014), 511.
2. Jack Henry Abbott, *In the Belly of the Beast: Letters from Prison* (New York: Random House, 1981), x–xi.

Chapter One

1. Jack Henry Abbott to Norman Mailer (hereafter abbreviated as "JHA" and "NM"), February 9, 1978 (Harry Ransom/Humanities Research Center, University of Texas at Austin; HRC below). All quotations from Abbott's letters to Mailer come from the papers in the HRC.
2. Samuel W. Smith to Senator Frank E. Moss (Utah), July 3, 1975 (HRC).
3. *Conversations with Jerzy Kosinski*, ed. Tom Teicholz (Jackson: University Press of Mississippi, 1993), 203–05.
4. Jack Henry Abbott, *In the Belly of the Beast: Letters from Prison* (New York: Random House, 1981), 18–19.

5. Jerome Loving, "The Father and Son of American Realism: The Second Acts of Dreiser and Mailer," *Mailer Review* (2013), 66–73; and J. Michael Lennon, *Norman Mailer: A Double Life* (New York: Simon & Schuster, 2013), 121.
6. *Selected Letters of Norman Mailer,* ed. J. Michael Lennon (New York: Random House, 2014), 505.
7. *In the Belly of the Beast*, 5.

Chapter Two

1. JHA to NM, May, 1982 (HRC).
2. Peter Manso, "Explosive Interview with Murderer Jack Henry Abbott," *Penthouse,* December 1982, 196–98.
3. JHA to NM, October 8, 1978 (HRC); and Jack Henry Abbott, *In the Belly of the Beast: Letters from Prison* (New York: Random House, 1981), 4.
4. Carl Rollyson, *The Lives of Norman Mailer* (New York: Paragon House, 1991), 1–4.
5. NM to Beatrice Silverman, April 11, 1944 (HRC).
6. Peter Manso, *Mailer: His Life and Times* (New York: Simon & Schuster, 1985), 329–30.
7. J. Michael Lennon, *Norman Mailer: A Double Life* (New York: Simon & Schuster, 2013), 190.
8. Alfred Kazin, "The Trouble He's Seen," *New York Times Book Review*, May 5, 1968.
9. *Selected Letters of Norman Mailer*, ed. J. Michael Lennon (New York: Random House, 2014), 516–17.

Chapter Three

1. William Styron, *This Quiet Dust* (New York: Random House, 1982), 112.
2. Thomas B. McElwee, *A Concise History of the Eastern Penitentiary of Pennsylvania* (Philadelphia: Neal and Massey, 1835), 15.
3. Ibid., 14.
4. Ibid., 16–18.

5. www.easternstate.org/learn/research-library/history.
6. www.victorianweb.org/authors/dickens/pva/pva344.html.
7. Michael Morton, *Getting Life: An Innocent Man's 25-Year Journey from Prison to Peace* (New York: Simon & Schuster, 2014), 127.
8. J. Michael Lennon, *Norman Mailer: A Double Life* (New York: Simon & Schuster, 2013), 168.
9. JHA to NM, September 24, 1978 (HRC).
10. Lennon, *Norman Mailer: A Double Life*, 563.
11. JHA to NM, February 7, 1983 (HRC).
12. Peter Manso, "Explosive Interview with Murderer Jack Henry Abbott," *Penthouse,* December 1982, 97.

Chapter Four

1. Jack Henry Abbott, *In the Belly of the Beast: Letters from Prison* (New York: Random House, 1981), 142–43; and Jack Henry Abbott, "The Case Reviewed in the Left-Communist Movement: Politics by Means of Law," c. 1982, unpublished typescript (HRC).
2. www.bop.gov/iloc2/InmateFinderServlet?Transaction=IDSearch&needingMoreList=false.
3. www.solitarywatch.com/2013/03/01/tracking-the-rise-of-solitary-confinement-in-america-and-of-the-struggle-against-it/.
4. *In the Belly of the Beast*, 30.
5. M. A. Farber, "Freedom for Convict-Author: Complex and Conflicting Tale," *New York Times*, August 17, 1981; and JHA to NM, May 20, 1980 (HRC).
6. Jack Henry Abbott, "The Case Reviewed in the Left-Communist Movement: Politics by Means of Law," c. 1982, unpublished typescript (HRC).
7. J. Michael Lennon, *Norman Mailer: A Double Life* (New York: Simon & Schuster, 2013), 552.
8. Farber, "Freedom for Convict-Author."
9. *In the Belly of the Beast*, 76.
10. Farber, "Freedom for Convict-Author."
11. JHA to NM, November 29, 1978 (HRC).

12. JHA to NM, December 8, 1978 (HRC).
13. *In the Belly of the Beast*, xvi.

Chapter Five

1. JHA to NM, November 7, 1979 (HRC).
2. "Billy Budd, Sailor (An Inside Narrative)," in *Herman Melville*, ed. Harrison Hayford (New York: Library of America, 1984), 1362–63.
3. Jack Henry Abbott with Naomi Zack, *My Return* (Buffalo: Prometheus Press, 1987), 184–85.
4. JHA to NM, February 18, 1982, and November 29, 1979 (HRC).
5. JHA to NM, November 29, 1979 (HRC).
6. NM to JHA, November 5, 1978 (HRC).
7. NM to JHA, May 10, 1978 (HRC).
8. JHA to NM, September 24, 1978 (HRC).
9. Steven Levy, "Fate Writes an Epilog to Prisoner's Book," *Philadelphia Bulletin,* September 10, 1981; and Norman Mailer, *The Executioner's Song: A True Life Novel* (Boston: Little, Brown, 1979), 353.
10. JHA to NM, October 1, 1978 (HRC).
11. J. Michael Lennon, *Norman Mailer: A Double Life* (New York: Simon & Schuster, 2013), 518–20.
12. Barry Farrell and Lawrence Schiller, "Gary Gilmore: A Series of Conversations, Ending on the Eve of His Execution, with the Utah Killer who Renewed the Capital-Punishment Debate by Demanding His Right to Die," *Playboy,* April 1977; also quoted in *The Executioner's Song,* 831.

Chapter Six

1. Transcript of NM press conference, Manhattan courthouse, January 21, 1982 (J. Michael Lennon Files).
2. Lee Bernstein, *America Is the Prison: Arts and Politics in Prison in the 1970s* (Chapel Hill: University of North Carolina Press, 2010), 151.
3. George Jackson, *Soledad Brother: The Prison Letters of George Jackson* (New York: Bantam Books, 1970), 23, 42.

4. Eldridge Cleaver, *Soul on Ice* (New York: McGraw-Hill, 1968), 17.
5. Angela Y. Davis, *Are Prisons Obsolete?* (New York: Seven Stories Press, 2003), 54–55.
6. Bernstein, *America Is the Prison*, 15–16.
7. Eric Mann, *Comrade George: An Investigation into the Life, Political Thought, and Assassination of George Jackson* (New York: Harper and Row, 1972), 40–42.
8. Jack Henry Abbott, "The Case Reviewed in the Left-Communist Movement: Politics by Means of Law," c. 1982, unpublished typescript (HRC).
9. Bernstein, *America Is the Prison*, 163–65.

Chapter Seven

1. Norman Mailer, *The Executioner's Song: A True Life Novel* (Boston: Little, Brown, 1979), 827.
2. Robert A. Ferguson, *Inferno: An Anatomy of American Punishment* (Cambridge: Harvard University Press, 2014), 140.
3. *Executioner's Song*, 820.
4. JHA to NM, October 8, 1978 (HRC); and *Autobiography of Malcolm X*, ed. Alex Haley (New York: Random House, 1964), 159.
5. *Executioner's Song*, 17.
6. JHA to NM, October 15 and February 9, 1978 (HRC). In a letter to the editor of *Newsweek* in early 1966, shortly after the publication of *In Cold Blood*, Mailer agreed that the novel was "great" but questioned whether it had been worth five years of Capote's talent: "While his killers are good, then unforgettable, his townspeople and cops sink from good to fair, and too many pages are pedestrian. Perhaps a novel composed entirely of certified facts must bury too much" (*Selected Letters of Norman Mailer*, ed. Michael J. Lennon [New York: Random House, 2014], 357).
7. Barry Farrell and Lawrence Schiller, "Gary Gilmore: A Series of Conversations, Ending on the Eve of His Execution, with the Utah Killer who Renewed the Capital-Punishment Debate by Demanding His Right to Die," *Playboy*, April 1977, 76, 80.

Chapter Eight

1. Norman Mailer, *The Executioner's Song: A True Life Novel* (Boston: Little, Brown, 1979), 224.
2. Ibid., 482.
3. Ibid., 25.
4. Jack H. Abbott, "Two Notes," *New York Review of Books*, June 11, 1981.
5. Interview of Bessie Gilmore, by Lawrence Schiller, July 31, 1977; and JHA to NM, December 11, 1978 (HRC).
6. JHA to NM, January 5, 1979 (HRC).

Chapter Nine

1. Mikal Gilmore, *Shot in the Heart* (New York: Anchor Books, 1995), 85. I am indebted to this prizewinning biography for much of the information in this chapter.
2. Ibid., 91.
3. Ibid., 96.
4. Ibid., 125, 143.
5. Ibid., 148, 147.
6. Ibid., 169.
7. Ibid., 251.
8. Interviews with Sterling Baker, April 2, 1978; Rikki Baker, March 5, 1977; and Bessie Gilmore, July 31, 1977 (HRC).

Chapter Ten

1. Interview with Rhoda Wolf, by J. Michael Lennon, February 10, 2010; J. Michael Lennon, *Norman Mailer: A Double Life* (New York: Simon and Schuster, 2013), 17.
2. Norman Mailer, *The Spooky Art: Thoughts on Writing* (Boston: Little, Brown, 2003), 6.
3. Norman Mailer, *The Naked and the Dead* (New York: New American Library, 1948, 1976), 175.
4. James T. Farrell, *Studs Lonigan* (New York: Signet, 1958), 359.

5. Robert K. Landers, *An Honest Writer: The Life and Times of James T. Farrell* (San Francisco: Encounter Books, 2004), 109; and Joseph Warren Beach, *American Fiction, 1920–1940* (New York: Russell and Russell, 1960), 280.
6. James T. Farrell, "A Novelist Begins," *Atlantic Monthly* 162, September 1938, 333.
7. Mikal Gilmore, *Shot in the Heart* (New York: Anchor Books, 1995), 111.
8. Norman Mailer, *The Executioner's Song: A True Life Novel* (Boston: Little, Brown, 1979), 5
9. Ibid., 10.
10. Ibid., 6.
11. Ibid., 115, 117
12. Ibid., 623, 890.
13. Ibid., 887.
14. Ibid., 913.
15. Ibid., 980.
16. Ibid., 986–88.
17. Ibid., 1048–49.
18. J. Michael Lennon to Jerome Loving, April 11, 2015.
19. *Selected Letters of Norman Mailer*, ed. J. Michael Lennon (New York: Random House, 2014), 530.

Chapter Eleven

1. "Norman Mailer: Letters to Jack Abbott," *New York Review of Books,* March 12, 2009.
2. Norman Mailer, *The Executioner's Song* (Boston: Little, Brown, 1979), 67; and JHA to NM, September 3, 1979 (HRC).
3. JHA to NM, October 5, 1979 (HRC).
4. J. Michael Lennon, *Norman Mailer: A Double Life* (New York: Simon & Schuster, 2013), 542; and Laurence Gonzales, *The Still Point* (Fayetteville: University of Arkansas Press, 1989), 173.
5. JHA to NM, November 6, 1979 (HRC).

Chapter Twelve

1. JHA to NM, November 7, 1979 (HRC).
2. JHA to NM, May 1, 1980 (HRC).
3. JHA to NM, August 3, 1980 (HRC).
4. JHA to NM, January 20, 1981 (HRC).
5. J. Michael Lennon, *Norman Mailer: A Double Life* (New York: Simon & Schuster, 2013), 550–51.
6. JHA to NM, February 17, 1981 (HRC).
7. JHA to NM, March 23, 1981 (HRC).
8. JHA to NM, April 5, 1981 (HRC).
9. JHA to NM, May 20, 1981 (HRC); and Mark Muro, "Jack's Letters to Norman," *Boston Globe*, September 14, 1987.
10. Robert Sam Anson, "The Brief and Violent Freedom of Jack Abbott," *Life,* November 1981, 124.

Chapter Thirteen

1. Norris Church Mailer, *A Ticket to the Circus; A Memoir* (New York: Random House, 2010), 264.
2. "Half Way House Unobtrusively Preparing Prisoners for Society," *New York Times*, August 11, 1981.
3. JHA to NM, February 18, 1982 (HRC); and Robert Sam Anson, "The Brief and Violent Freedom of Jack Abbott," *Life,* November, 1981, taken from draft in JHA-NM correspondence, HRC File 677.2
4. Norris Church Mailer, *Ticket to the Circus*, 264–65.
5. Ibid., 268.
6. NM to Michael Adams, November 25, 1981, in *Selected Letters of Norman Mailer*, ed. J. Michael Lennon (New York: Random House, 2014), 549.
7. Steven Levy, "Fate Writes an Epilog to Prisoner's Book," *Philadelphia Bulletin*, September 10, 1981; and J. Michael Lennon, *Norman Mailer: A Double Life* (New York: Simon & Schuster, 2013), 553–54, 556.
8. JHA to NM, June 1, 1982 (HRC).
9. Norris Church Mailer, *Ticket to the Circus*, 265.

10. Telephone interview with Erroll McDonald, July 31, 2015.
11. Telephone interviews with Gary Fisketjon, October 29, 2015, and October 30, 2015.
12. Telephone interview with Robert Silvers, August 19, 2015.
13. M. A. Farber, "Killing Clouds Ex-Convict Writer's New Life," *New York Times*, July 26, 1981.
14. JHA to NM, May 1982.
15. Lisa Phu, "A Widow's Journey through Grief, Anger and Art," www.ktoo.org/2015/03/19/widows-journey-grief-anger-art/.
16. Jerome Loving, interview with William Majeski, Algonquin Hotel, New York, NY, October 13, 2014. When Detective Majeski reread this description of Abbott, he commented: "If I used this term I must be mellowing. It is clearly the kindest reference I have ever made about a despicable, depraved, cunning fabricator who should never [have] been released back into society."
17. Paul L. Montgomery, "Witness in Abbott Trial Tells of Night of Murder," *New York Times*, January 14, 1982.
18. Peter Manso, "Explosive Interview with Murderer Jack Henry Abbott," *Penthouse,* December, 1982, 98.

Chapter Fourteen

1. Jack Henry Abbott, *In the Belly of the Beast: Letters from Prison* (New York: Random House, 1981), 3.
2. Ibid., 3.
3. Ibid., 7.
4. Ibid., 10.
5. Ariel Levy, "The Price of a Life," *New Yorker*, April 13, 2015.
6. *In the Belly of the Beast*, 14.
7. Ibid., 20.
8. Ibid., 40.
9. Ibid., 43–45.
10. Ibid., 66, 68, 75.
11. Anon., "Survey of Books Relating to the Law," *Michigan Law Review,* 81.4 (March, 1983), 1219–26.

Chapter Fifteen

1. Terrence Des Pres, "A Child of the State: *In the Belly of the Beast*," *New York Times Book Review*, July 19, 1981.
2. M. A. Farber, "The Detective vs. The Fugitive: How Jack Abbott Was Found," *New York Times*, October 11, 1981.
3. JHA to NM, June 1, 1982 (HRC).
4. Peter Manso, *Mailer: His Life and Times* (New York: Simon and Schuster, 1985), 632.
5. J. Michael Lennon, *Norman Mailer: A Double Life* (New York: Simon & Schuster, 2013), 559–60.
6. Jack Henry Abbott with Naomi Zack, *My Return* (Buffalo: Prometheus Books, 1987), 95; and interview of Majeski, by Jerome Loving, October 13, 2014.
7. J. Michael Lennon, *Norman Mailer: A Double Life*, 559–60; and Dean Brelis, "In New York: Tracking a Murder Suspect," *Time*, October 26, 1981, 14.
8. Paul L. Montgomery, "Jury Starts Deliberating in the Abbott Murder Case," *New York Times*, January 21, 1981.
9. Lennon, *Norman Mailer: A Double Life*, 562–63.
10. Press conference, Manhattan courthouse, January 21, 1982 (HRC).
11. Mailer Collection, HRC File 254.2.

Chapter Sixteen

1. Frank Coffey, *60 Minutes: 25 Years of Television's Finest Hour* (Los Angeles: General Publishing Group, 1993), 217–18.
2. *60 Minutes,* Transcript of interview, CBS, April 18, 1982 / February 17, 2002.
3. James Atlas, "The Literary Life of Crime," *New Republic*, September 9, 1981, 21–23.
4. Ibid., 23; and J. Michael Lennon, *Norman Mailer: A Double Life* (New York: Simon & Schuster, 2013), 565.
5. Lance Morrow, "The Poetic License to Kill," *Time*, February 1, 1982, 82.

6. Coffey, *60 Minutes*, 128. In reconstructing this interview, I am indebted to Coffey's book as well as to Vicki Gordon, executive story editor for *60 Minutes* at CBS for a transcript of the interview, and to the Robert Vincent Voice Library, Michigan State University, for an audio of the interview. I also indebted to Mary Loving for putting me in touch with Vicki Gordon.

Chapter Seventeen

1. www.ktoo.org/2015/03/19/widows-journey-grief-anger-art/. JHA to Hilary Mills Loomis, June 26, 1982 (HRC); and Gioia Diliberto, "Jack Abbott's Other Victims Fight Back, Suing for the Royalties That Came with His Fame," *People*, February 8, 1982.
2. Jennifer Gonnerman, "Before the Law," *New Yorker,* October 6, 2014, 26–32.
3. Ibid., 32.
4. "Kalief Browder, Held at Rikers Island for 3 Years Without Trial, Commits Suicide," *New York Times*, June 9, 2015.
5. Abbott, *In the Belly of the Beast*, 25, 45–46.
6. JHA to NM, May, 1982 (HRC).
7. JHA to Larry Flynt, November 24, 1982 (HRC).
8. Peter Manso, "Explosive Interview with Murderer Jack Henry Abbott," *Penthouse,* December 1982, 200.

Chapter Eighteen

1. Jack Henry Abbott, "The Case Reviewed in the Left-Communist Movement: Politics by Means of Law," c. 1982, unpublished typescript (HRC).
2. "Esteemed Journalist Akinshiju C. Ola Passes," *New York Amsterdam News*, February 13, 2002.
3. *Selected Letters of Norman Mailer*, ed. J. Michael Lennon (New York: Random House, 2014), 549.
4. JHA to NM, July 24, 1982 (HRC).
5. J. Michael Lennon, *Norman Mailer: A Double Life* (New York: Simon & Schuster, 2013), 571–73; *Selected Letters*, 606, 692–93,

815n; and Nora Ephron et al., "The Farber Case," *New York Review of Books*, July 16, 1987.

6. Lennon, *Norman Mailer: A Double Life*, 619–20.
7. *Selected Letters*, 576.
8. Jack Henry Abbott with Naomi Zack, *My Return* (Buffalo: Prometheus Books, 1987), xi–xii.
9. Lennon, *Norman Mailer: A Double Life*, 619–20; *Selected Letters*, 603; Abbott with Zack, *My Return*, 123.
10. www.thesmokinggun.com/file/jack-henry-abbott-goes-out-print?page=1.
11. "Jailhouse Author Helped by Mailer Is Found Dead," *New York Times*, February 11, 2002.
12. *Selected Letters*, 570–71.
13. NM to Sharon Churcher, September 26, 1993 (HRC).
14. *Selected Letters*, 622.

Index